CHICAGO PUBLIC LIBRARY
BUSINESS / SCIENCE / TECHNOLOGY
400 S. STATE ST

CHICAGO PUBLIC LIBRARY
BUSINESS / SCIENCE / TECHNOLOGY
400 S. STATE ST   C0C05

CHICAGO PUBLIC LIBRARY
BUSINESS / SCIENCE / TECHNOLOGY
400 S. STATE ST. 60605

CHICAGO PUBLIC LIBRARY

R00978 39393

Chicago Public Library

Form 178 rev. 11-00

CHICAGO PUBLIC LIBRARY
BUSINESS / SCIENCE / TECHNOLOGY
400 S. STATE ST.   60605

"When we tug at a single thing in Nature—
we find it attached to the rest of the world"

John Muir

THE HOLISTIC GARDEN

Birds eye view of the Garden

THE
HOLISTIC
GARDEN

a simple guide to a safe, fruitful,
ecologically-balanced landscape

by

Barbara Allen

Illustrated by Faun Parliman
Cover Mandala by Bryon Allen
Edited by Elizabeth Daniels

Published by
Essential Sources
Eugene, OR

All rights reserved. No part of this book may be reproduced or transmitted in any form
or by any means, electronic or mechanical, including photocopying, recording or by
any information storage and retrieval system without written permission from the
author, except for the inclusion of brief quotations in a review.

Other books by the author
Gardening Naturally

Copyright © 1993 by Barbara Allen
Illustrations copyright © 1993 by Faun Parliman
Cover illustration copyright © 1993 by Bryon Allen
Illustrations on pages 7, 8, 15, 17, 99, 110 and
"Bird's Eye View of the Garden" copyright © 1993 by Barbara Allen

First Printing Nov.1993
Second Printing Jan.1994

The author and publishers will be grateful for any information which will assist them in
keeping future editions up to date. Although all reasonable care has been taken in the
preparation of this book, neither the publishers nor the author can accept any liability for
any consequences arising from the use thereof, or from the information contained herein.

ISBN 0-9635421-0-9

AGO PUBLIC LIBRARY
NESS / SCIENCE / TECHNOLOGY
. STATE ST.   60605 _59_ F

R00978 39393

For my husband and best friend Bruce,
whose love, encouragement and hours of patient
editing and proof-reading made this possible.

"Come forth into the light of things,
Let Nature be your teacher."

William Wordsworth

Acknowledgments

Special thanks to my parents who made me believe anything was possible and to our children Laurie, Bryon and Daniel and all those good friends who encouraged, supported and helped make this book happen; to Faun for her faith in my vision and her patience and endurance in creating the lovely art that brings life to this book, to Bryon for bringing forth the beautiful mandala for the cover, to Elizabeth for her careful and loving editing work and the words that first made me realize it was indeed a "book"! Thanks to Steve Du Bois for generously sharing his computer and his knowledge and especially to André Angermann for all his pains-taking and dedicated work and to Melissa Verbena for her loving energy, enthusiasm and hours of proof-reading. Harriet Kofalk and Alan Kapular each read the early manuscript and added their own special flavoring to it. Thank you, Daniel, for all your varied and caring contributions to the process, and to Mark, (thanks for the idea!) Leorra, Lorraine, Linda and all the other people who shared in the process and added something of themselves to it, I offer my heartfelt thanks and appreciation. It was an amazing group effort!

NSO HORTICULTURE
488 / SCIENCE TECHNOLOGY
STATE ST.   00000

TABLE OF CONTENTS

Preface

Preface

A delightful new vision of the world is rising softly over our horizon—a vision that finds the planet no longer revolving with humanity at its center, but rather in the midst of an enormous orchestra, each instrument played by a different life form from the smallest single-celled creature to the planet itself. Each playing a vastly marvelous complex symphony in perfect harmony together.

Awakening on stage we realize that we are not the conductor but simply one of the musicians and we are not playing the same tune as everyone else! We have been playing out of tune and out of time.

In startled embarrassment we stand silent, listening as the music flows around us, each of our fellow musicians playing in perfect synchronicity. Slowly, we begin to sense the part we play, and shyly—softly at first—we sound our note, testing its appropriateness. As we hear the quiet harmony with which it rings, our confidence grows. Joy flows through us, as our note rings clear in perfect harmony with the rest, resonating, lifting...

Like children, humankind has seen the world revolving about themselves. The day has come that we must set aside our "childish toys" and awake to our adult role on this planet. It is a wondrous place in which we live, an incredibly complex living system and we are just beginning to look around us to seek the part we play in it all. It is an exciting journey of discovery and we can begin it right here and now, in our own backyard. We can create a safe and healthy environment for a multitude of life forms, from the bacteria in our soil to the birds in our trees, an environment that respects the existence of each form it finds there and the part each plays in the web of life.

Introduction

Although we have gardened organically for nearly 35 years - few of the families for whom I created nearly 700 landscape designs were familiar with the organic approach. There was little information available. Back in 1978 I began to put together a simple planting and maintenance guide for my clients that offered environmentally friendly alternatives to the usual garden products and practices. An expanded and updated version called "Gardening Naturally" was published in 1990 by Oregon Tilth, an educational organization that certifies organic farms in Oregon.

"The Holistic Garden" book goes beyond simple organic practices. It embraces the growing understanding that we are not alone on this planet. Our lives and gardens are related to and dependent on the lives of myriad creatures and plants whose names and faces we may not even know.

My aim has been to gather together the *essence* of the latest ideas and information on environmentally sound gardening practices (I have also included a section on the *design* process as I feel this is a most useful tool for the home gardener). With such information we feel we can begin to make some serious changes in the world around us.

For those who prefer a more visual experience, I created the story of a family and the "holistic" garden they created. Part of this story begins each chapter, followed by the more "nuts and bolts" information. The landscape designs and drawings are all based on this garden. The chapter on wildlife was written from the "point of view" of a bat who resides there.

Of course, the most important step of all involves a change of *attitude*. A change to one that takes into account the welfare of the planet and the multitude of life forms that share it with us. If we ask ourselves how each action we take in our lives and in our gardens may affect this intricate web of life we can begin to make a real difference. With backyard gardeners around the planet asking the same question we can begin to do some real environmental healing.

Barbara and Bruce Allen

Planning Your Garden

2

Planning Your Garden

Schemes and Dreams and Endless Possibilities

This yard will be different. No longer are you willing to be a slave to lawns and flower beds, fruit trees and weeds. You love gardening, but you are never more at peace than when you are in natural places: meadows and forests, mountains and ocean beaches. You determined that here you would create a more "natural" garden—a garden you could become a part of, where you could work with nature to achieve the kind of balance you have seen in the wild. It will be a learning process you know, for you still want to grow vegetables and have fruit to nibble right from the tree or bush. But you know you wouldn't enjoy the results of just sitting back and letting the grass and weeds grow and letting nature "do its thing"(lawn grasses are not, after all, natural here).

When you first saw the open sunny area behind the chicken house, you knew this could be your meadow, a place for wildflowers and grasses to grow for birds and butterflies and bees, and sweeping around it on two sides is a grove of mature trees, well on its way to becoming a woodland.

That is all easy to see, but you know from past experience that without a plan, a framework in which to create your garden, you might end up with an unlovely hodge-podge. You had felt in the past that not planning would make a garden more natural—but in fact this did not turn out to be the case. Your life in the past was filled with weedy paths and overcrowded plants and soil that was tired and hard. Whatever it takes, you will not plant anything at your new home until you can give it a rich healthy soil to grow in. And you will make sure to give each plant the other things they need as well, like room to grow without pruning, and the amount of sun each needs to do its best. All these things you had been ignorant of in the past until it was too late for many of your plants.

The weak plants had been plagued by bugs and disease and spraying only seemed to make it worse in the end. Then you read how much birds and other insect-eating creatures can help to maintain balance in the bug population in your yard. You stopped spraying (it was harming *those* creatures too) and started doing things to invite them into your yard. It had taken time but before you moved you had begun to see an obvious improvement. You and your family had become fascinated bird watchers in the process, running for the bird book each time a new species showed up at the feeder or bird bath. You read together about all the night flying insects that bats and screech owls will eat and about toads, snakes, shrews and skunks, wasps, spiders and other wildlife that help maintain balance in the insect population, and you found out what you could do to create habitat for them and make them feel safe and welcome. You would study the area to be sure you didn't destroy any existing native plants or habitat.

A pond will be an important part of the plan and you found a low boggy area at the new place that seems a very natural environment for a pond. Your catalogs tell you there are even some lovely fruiting plants that like boggy soil (not many do!). You will use native wetland plants, too, like rushes and sedges.

You researched groundcovers you can use in place of lawn. The front lawn here is small and too near the street for play so you plan to replace it all with something more interesting and useful and easier to care for. White Dutch clover stays low and green with only 1 or 2 mowings a year and needs little water because of its very deep roots. Honeybees and butterflies love it and the mowings will add nutrients to your compost pile. Birdsfoot trefoil is another groundcover you can seed and besides being especially beautiful in bloom it is an important butterfly and insect plant. The lawn you leave in back for the kids to play on will be overseeded with one of the new slow growing, drought-tolerant flowering lawn seed mixes.

With the ready availability of the more common fruits you decided to concentrate on more unusual and care-free plants like persimmon and pawpaw. Many of the food plants you chose are enjoyed by wildlife as well. Your vegetable garden will be near the house and have permanent weed-proof paths and boxed raised beds that will make it attractive and easy to care for.

You know that even with a plan it will all take time to put together. It will need extra care until things become established and able to care for themselves. You realize that with a plan you and nature can work together to bring balance and harmony to this small part of the planet.

PUTTING IT ON PAPER

Although building healthy active soil may be the most important thing you do in your yard, the FIRST thing you should do is create a plan. The primary purpose of a plan is to help identify the priorities for your outdoor space and choose the best places for those activities to occur. Then you can determine how many plants and features (patio, play area, compost bins, etc.) you can comfortably fit in the space available. A plan will save wasted space, time, money and overcrowded plants.

DON'T PANIC! You can do this! All it takes is a couple free afternoons (tough one, I know!) and the following items:

a.   2-3 sheets of 24" x 30", 8 squares to the inch graph paper*

b.   25'-50' measuring tape

c.   a pencil and eraser

d.   a ruler

e.   2-3 sheets of 24" x 30" tracing paper*

f.   scratch paper—letter size

*The graph and tracing paper can be found at your local blueprint or art supply shop.

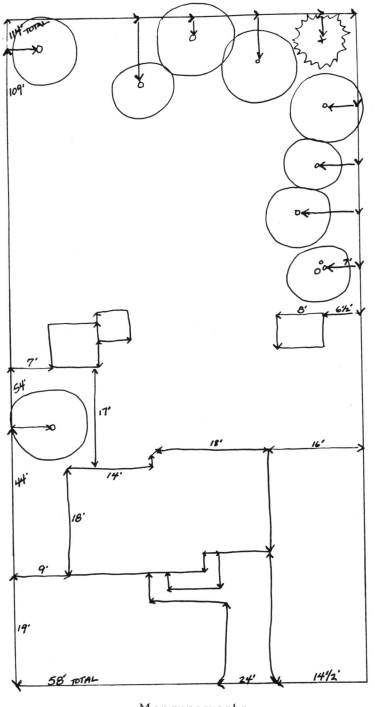

Measurements

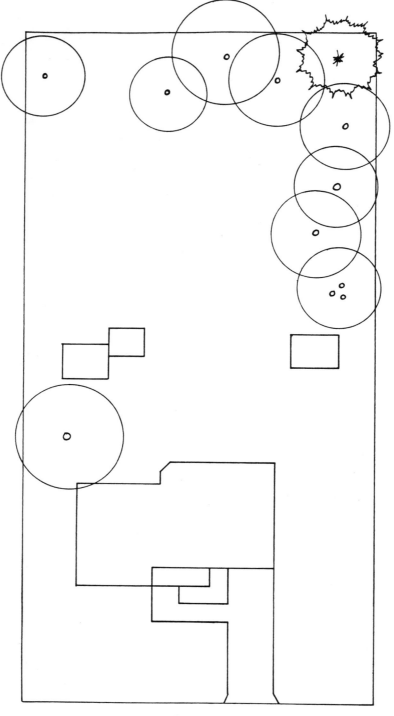

The Base Plan

STEP BY STEP

Drawing the Base Plan

1. With your pad of scratch paper, your pencil and measuring tape in hand head out to your yard. Make a rough sketch of all the main features in your landscape—property lines, house, driveway, walks, existing trees, etc. Starting with the longest straightest property line, take measurements as shown on the sketch. Take your time, and get measurements from two directions (at right angles) for each corner and feature.

2. Note the movement of the sun through your yard during the day. Mark *North, South, East* and *West*.

3. Note the views from various places inside the house and out, especially good ones as well as especially bad ones.

4. Decide which existing plants you want to keep and which could go, working as you go to preserve native species and habitat (such as wetland, woodland, etc.).

5. Take your measurements to a big, well lit table and tape your graph paper in front of you.

6. Using your rough sketch, start translating your measurements onto the graph paper starting with the property boundaries. On your drawing each little square equals one foot. Simple, huh? If your property is 50'x100', that's 50 squares by 100 squares.

7. Draw in the house exactly as it sits on the property, making dots for each of the corners first and connecting them when you are done.

8. Finish adding the main features using my sketch as a guide. If something isn't working right, go out and check your measurements for that spot again.

***If you have a very complex house and yard, or just feel you don't have the time or inclination to do this part, you can hire a landscape designer to do it for you.

NOW, with the help of the rest of the family, fill out the forms on the following pages, then sit in a comfy chair—preferably out in your existing garden—and take a journey through a holistic garden and discover how you can create one for yourself.

QUESTIONS TO ASK:

← What wild plants, animals and their habitat, such as meadows, woods and wetlands, exist here already and how can I best preserve these?_____

← What can we do to make this a better habitat for other life forms?_____

← Do we need more shade for a part of our house or yard?___Where?_____

← Do we need a windbreak for some area?_____ Where?_____

← Do we have a great view to preserve?_____ Where?_____

← Do we have a terrible one we want to screen?_____ Where?_____

← Do we need more privacy?_____For the whole yard or just a part?_____Which part?_____

← Do we need to keep pets, small children, or wildlife in or out of our yard?_____

← Do we need more room for parking? (Vehicles are a part of life even in a natural landscape!)_____ For bicycles, R.V.s, boats, etc.?_____

THINGS TO KEEP IN MIND

✛ Wildlife and existing native plants and their needs.

✛ The sun's movement through your yard during the day and throughout the seasons.

✛ Whether the plants you want will not only get enough sun **now** but *five years* from now.

✛ The size your plants will be 5 to 10 years from now. Will everything have enough room to grow without pruning?

✛ Underground water/ gas/ electric/ phone lines. There's a number you can call to have them all marked for you before you start digging. Check the telephone book under Phone Services.

✛ Natural foot traffic patterns.

✛ Pets—yours and your neighbors. How they will affect your plantings.

✛ Water usage and availability.

LIST OF POSSIBLE FEATURES

◆ Flowers for butterflies and insects
◆ Flowers for cutting/ eating/ smelling
◆ Woodland garden/ Native species/ Endangered species
◆ Food for critters
◆ Patio/ Deck/ Sitting area
◆ Children's play area
◆ Greenhouse/ cold frame
◆ Vegetable garden
◆ Fruit trees and bushes
◆ Fish pond
◆ Herbs
◆ Meadow/ Wild Garden
◆ Compost bins
◆ Recycling bins
◆ Tool storage
◆ Bike/ Boat/ R.V. storage
◆ Potting shed/ Utility area
◆ Fire pit
◆ Swimming pool
◆ Hot tub
◆ Songbird garden
◆ Birdbath
◆ Birdfeeder
◆ Meditation area
◆ Chicken/ Rabbit pens
◆ Heirloom species garden
◆ Medicinal plant garden
◆ Soccer/ Badminton/ Volleyball

LIST OF PLANTS WE'D REALLY LIKE TO GROW

Look at the plant lists throughout this book for ideas or, if you are really unfamiliar with plants and their names, take a walk through your local nursery or peruse a couple of good plant books from the library.

PLANT NAME	ULTIMATE SIZE	NEEDS SUN OR SHADE	OTHER SPECIAL NEEDS

MICRO-CLIMATES

In order to utilize the space you have to its fullest you will want to take a close look at what are called "micro-climates" in your landscape. For example the area next to the **south** wall of a house might have a warmer "climate" than the area near a **north** facing wall. Fences, building walls and dense hedges create protected areas. These can be used for plants needing more heat or protection from cold than the general climate of your area. This might allow you to grow a plant that would not otherwise do well in your zone. (i.e. A tomato plant grown in the Pacific Northwest, where summers can be cool and wet, has a better chance of producing ripe fruit if planted near a sunny south facing wall.) On the other hand compost doesn't need sun to work, so a damp shady spot behind the garage could be used for it, although mint, ferns and wintergreen might be happy there too. If you have a spot that is too shady for vegetables, try a woodland garden with native plants and a few wild edibles like pawpaw, serviceberry and highbush cranberry, or huckleberries, lingonberry and wild strawberries. The birds will appreciate it as well.

Note any area that gets a great deal of wind during any season and be certain the plants that you put there will take this in their stride. A hot, dry bank will be a happy home for some plants and slow death for others; just as a low boggy spot would be "home sweet home" for some. More than likely you will find plants available in your area that will be happy in every "microclimate" in your landscape. Make notes on your plan of the special areas and find plants that are suited to each.

USE ZONES

Many areas and features and plants can be combined in one "use zone". For example:

- Utility/potting shed/compost bins/rabbit hutch/clothesline

- Meditation area/fish pond/woodland garden/birdbath

- Children's play area/grape arbor/picnic table/fruit bushes

- Privacy screen/ "bad view" screen/ windbreak/ "fruit fence"

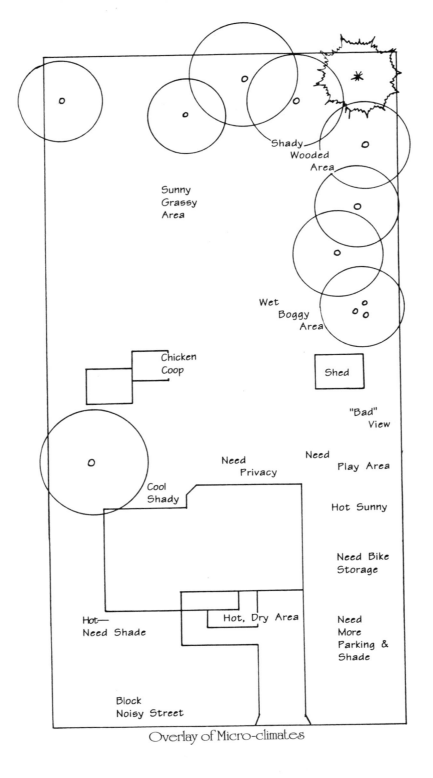

Shady
Wooded
Area

Sunny
Grassy
Area

Wet
Boggy
Area

Chicken
Coop

Shed

"Bad"
View

Need
Privacy

Need
Play Area

Cool
Shady

Hot Sunny

Need Bike
Storage

Hot—
Need Shade

Hot, Dry Area

Need
More
Parking &
Shade

Block
Noisy Street

Overlay of Micro-climates

HIGH AND LOW ATTENTION AREAS

Your property may also be separated into areas needing frequent attention and those needing little attention. For the most part, areas needing daily care should be located nearest the house, with the exception of chickens and rabbits (the potential for odiferousness on a hot summer day is great, no matter how clean you may keep them!).

HIGH ATTENTION AREAS:

- ❖ Frequently harvested veggies—lettuce, spinach, tomatoes, beans.
- ❖ Frequently harvested fruits—blueberries, strawberries.
- ❖ Often used herbs—thyme, basil, parsley.
- ❖ Flowers for close up viewing and fragrance—sweet alyssum, lavender, lilac.
- ❖ Birdfeeder and birdbath for viewing from patio and living room, and for refilling.
- ❖ Recycling bins.
- ❖ Play area for very young children.

LOW ATTENTION AREAS:

- ❖ Infrequently harvested veggies and fruits—potatoes, corn, Jerusalem artichokes, rhubarb, drying beans.
- ❖ Low-care fruit and nut trees.
- ❖ Compost bins.
- ❖ Wildflower meadow.
- ❖ Woodland garden.

Note these on your tissue overlay.

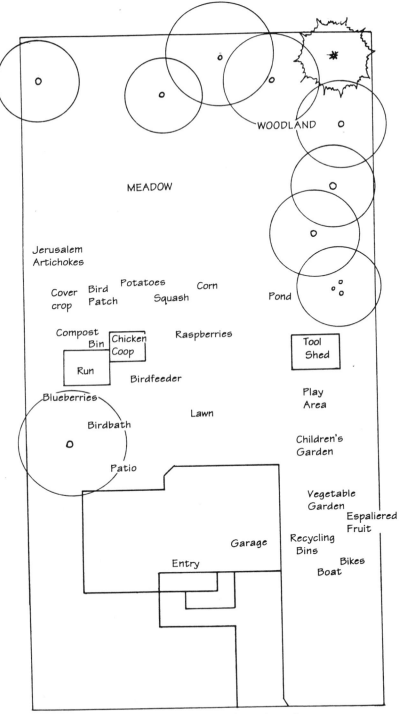

WOODLAND

MEADOW

Jerusalem
Artichokes

Cover   Bird   Potatoes   Corn
crop   Patch   Squash   Pond

Compost   Raspberries
Bin   Chicken
Coop   Tool
Run   Shed
            Birdfeeder
Blueberries   Play
                                             Area
      Birdbath
                        Lawn   Children's
                                             Garden

      Patio   Vegetable
                                             Garden
                                                   Espaliered
                                                   Fruit
                                             Recycling
                              Garage   Bins
                                                   Bikes
            Entry   Boat

Overlay of High and Low Attention Areas

17

DESIGNING FOR LOW MAINTENANCE

A. Keep it simple!

B. Use gentle flowing curves for areas that need mowing.

C. Emulate nature with meadows, woodlands, hedgerows, ponds, bogs and wetland areas, etc. Become a Garden Caretaker: make a place for nature to grow and add a little here, subtract a little there; aid the less aggressive and subdue the more aggressive; and bring the greatest possible diversity to your landscape.

D. Choose and place plants carefully. In selecting plants for a sustainable landscape:

1. **Use native plants** and naturally drought-tolerant, insect and disease-resistant plants, as they require the least attention.

2. **Place plants with care** to their needs for sun and moisture. Attention to their ultimate size and shape will result in little special care and little, if any, pruning.

3. **Choose plants for multiple functions.**

E. Keep lawn areas to a minimum, using grass only where it is needed for play, etc. and then use the new dwarf, drought-tolerant grasses. Use gentle curves for easier mowing. Substitute ground-covers on slopes, under trees and in front yards.

LABOR-SAVING TECHNIQUES

- **Mulch bare ground;** it cuts down on water needs and weeding chores and feeds soil critters.

- **Edge lawns with brick or paving** at soil level, to eliminate edging chores.

- **Use groundcovers** on bare soil under shrubs and trees to cut down on weeds.

- **Provide shelter, water and food for birds and other wildlife** to cut down on insect problems.

- **Use drought-tolerant plants** to cut down on watering needs.

- **Use timed drip and "ooze" watering systems,** where watering is needed, (especially in vegetable gardens) for the most efficient use of water and time.

- **Use plants native to your area** to create a more natural setting. Natives require little or no care.

- **Create permanent weed-proof paths** wherever possible, using weed-barrier cloth, deep gravel, concrete, brick, flagstones and other hard surfaces.

THE DROUGHT-TOLERANT, LOW-WATER-USAGE PLANTING

The finite amount of water on our planet must be used carefully by all of us, not just those presently suffering the effects of drought. Water is a non-renewable resource, just like oil. Some of the things we can do are:

*   Use drought-tolerant plants.

*   Plan landscapes with water conservation in mind.

*   Build moisture-retaining soils full of humus.

*   Reduce lawn areas and switch to the new deep-rooted, drought-tolerant grasses or a meadow lawn.

*   Use drip and "ooze" watering systems where watering is needed.

*   Use mulch on any bare soil.

*   Plant groundcovers which demand little water such as; creeping thyme, pussy-toes, clover, chamomile and trefoil.

*   Group heavy water users together for more efficient use of water.

A LIST OF QUESTIONS TO ASK OF EACH PLANT

1. Is it **INSECT AND DISEASE-RESISTANT** for our area? Local nursery people and Extension Services can often help with this question.

2. Is it **HARDY** and suited to our climate? Unless you want to experiment, choose plants for their ecological fitness to your site.

3. How **TALL** and **WIDE** will it get? Given enough room to grow, a plant will never need to be pruned because it's too big!

4. Is it **DROUGHT-RESISTANT**? Even in areas not normally bothered by drought, the problem may arise from time to time. A landscape with drought-tolerant plants will suffer less and make fewer demands on their caretaker (see Appendices).

5. What does it need to be **HAPPY**? Sun? Shade? Good drainage? Lots of moisture? A happy plant is healthy and thriving, needing little attention.

6. Is it **MESSY** at some time of the year? Does it drop fruit, twigs, sap, seed pods, etc.? This may be good for wildlife, but bad for patios, walkways and parking areas.

7. Is it **DECIDUOUS or EVERGREEN**? An evergreen tree casts shade in *winter* too. Does that work for you? An evergreen hedge gives you privacy all year long, not just in spring and summer, and provides shelter for overwintering creatures.

8. What **FUNCTIONS** will it have? Each plant should have at least **TWO.** Here are some possibilities:

Food for humans	Medicine
Food for critters	Compost material
Shade	Windbreak
Wildlife shelter	Pollution control
Cover crop	Noise barrier
Fragrance	Cut flowers
Privacy	Syrup
Erosion control	Firewood
Beauty	Nitrogen fixer
Species preservation	Other

9. Is it **SELF-SEEDING, SUCKERING OR INVASIVE** in any way? Self-seeding is an important attribute in a meadow plant, suckering is useful for a hedge, tree or shrub, but in some situations both are simply a maintenance headache!

10. Does it need **PRUNING**? Many fruit trees, bramble berries, groundcovers and vines need *yearly* pruning to look or do their best. Keep the number of these plants to a minimum.

11. Does it need frequent **STAKING, DIVIDING OR SPRAYING**? Avoid these plants when possible.

EVALUATE AND PRIORITIZE

Now, evaluate your answers on each of the plants you chose. Make sure that there will be a balance created in bringing each into your landscape. It may take some research and time spent questioning nursery people, growers and experienced gardeners in your area, but it will save an enormous amount of effort and time in the future.

List your absolute priorities of features and plants. Try not to get too carried away to begin with. After all, growing all your own food and holding down a full-time job might be unrealistic. Many "free" foods are available from wild plants, like blackberries and huckleberries, as well as excess apples, walnuts or zucchini from your friends and neighbors gardens. Use low-maintenance and native plants primarily, and install low-water usage watering systems as you go.

LIST PRIORITIES:

TALK TO EXPERIENCED GARDENERS IN YOUR AREA and get a sense of the time and effort involved in caring for various aspects of the garden you'd like to have. You will find:

○ A small fish pond demands little attention once established, but a row of espaliered apple trees needs pruning 2-3 times a year and possible attention to insects and disease problems as well.

○ Raspberries need regular tying and thinning and pruning, while blueberries need little more than an annual mulching.

○ A full-sized grape vine on an arbor will demand several hours winter pruning each year, whereas a persimmon tree will give you shade and fruit with much less effort.

BUT—If you really love apples, raspberries or grapes and can't wait to grow your own, the little extra effort needed will be well rewarded.

Start slowly with the higher maintenance plants, adding a few each year. If you take on more than you can handle well, you will get discouraged by possibly unsatisfactory results. Give yourself time to learn, to get the feel of a new kind of gardening. As time goes by you will find you can do more and more in less time, and by taking on new plants and projects slowly you will find yourself becoming more enthusiastic as your proficiency expands (fortunately, many *fruit* plants take 2-3 years before they need much more than mulch and water). Gardening is not some mysterious art that only people with the mystical "green thumb" can do. All you need is an attitude of respect and caring for your environment and other life forms, a desire to learn, and some very basic information.

The Bench under the Elderberry

24

The Holistic* Garden

*Holistic—Pertaining to the whole, excluding no parts

Ladybugs, Blueberries and Lavender

Ladybugs, blueberries, lavender, swallows, broccoli, earthworms—all part of a garden; a holistic garden. You are part of it, too. You are the chef that blends and mixes, adds and takes away, until you, the bugs, plants, birds and other critters have each settled comfortably into your own special places. You mix with a light and loving hand and allow the ingredients to guide you. A few more birds here, just a pinch of herbs there, a toad under the rhubarb; garter snake sunning near a cabbage, bats asleep in the shed; compost cooking in the corner.

Buckwheat blooms in last year's corn patch and honeybees make the clover under the persimmon tree sing in the morning sun. You harvested herbs after the dew dried and now enjoy a quiet cup of tea under the elderberry. The meadow will need mowing soon, but right now watching robins splash in the shallow end of the pond occupies all your attention. You watch the young ones learning to pull their own worms from your tiny patch of flowery lawn. Mole may make ridges in it in his search for worms, but the work he does on the soil underneath more than makes up for this.

A dainty mud dauber wasp works the wet spot under the faucet you left dripping for Toad. She and her family make quiet neighbors in the eaves over the back door. She stays busy filling her nest with insects for her larvae and seems not to mind your comings and goings. You haven't noticed as many flies in the house this year. She probably helped.

Toad has just galumped down that slug he's been watching for the last hour, the slug that was heading for the lettuce patch. Some new butterflies have just "hatched" in the garden. You saw the caterpillars working on the milkweed in the bean patch. You left the milkweed there in the hope that they would find it. The butterflies are enjoying the Phlox and black-eyed susans you planted especially for them.

The new filbert hedge back by the meadow is beginning to take hold. The family of squirrels that lives in your little woodland garden will be delighted when they discover the nuts it will bear in the next couple of years. There should be more than enough nuts for all of you.

The bug problem in the fruit trees is a thing of the past now that the bats have taken up residence in the house you built for them. The birds get the daytime bugs and the bats get the night flyers. Of course, Toad and Snake and the Ladybugs do their share. And so do the wasps and the dragonflies that visit your lily pond. You had a lot of bug problems before they all came. The pond attracted some of these helpful friends and so did the things you planted with them in mind. And there were other things, like the brush pile you left by the back fence and the wildflower meadow you planted three years ago.

The tiny woodland garden of native plants that you created so carefully, has fruit and shelter for the birds who winter there. Some of them prefer the millet and sunflowers you let go to seed at the edge of the meadow. They like your blueberries, too. That is why you built a frame of netting over them. The birds got carried away and forgot to leave any for you! They love the mulberries by the chicken run even better, though. (So far, none of their purple "bombs" have hit your laundry, but they did get the car once or twice. Maybe if you didn't park under the chestnut tree, where they sit after their mulberry lunch...)

It's all starting to work now. It's been three years since you tilled the vegetable garden. Mulching with compost each summer has made the soil in the raised beds so soft you can stick your hand right down into it!

You don't need to buy fertilizer anymore. Compost spread around 'most everything, every year or so seems to be all that's needed. You have enough compost since you started growing that patch of birdsfoot trefoil and using it and the clover mowing from under the persimmon tree. Then there's the extra comfrey from the bed by the chicken house. The chickens eat most of the comfrey, but they contribute wonderfully to the compost pile.

The worm bin in the laundry room works really well for composting kitchen scraps. Such a simple thing! Just a big covered plastic box, filled with shredded newspaper and a handful of "red wigglers." At first, this was just for winter. But, it was such a handy place for vegetable scraps from the kitchen that you just kept it going. The compost they make of the scraps and paper goes around your house-plants and they never looked so good!

You still have to prune the apple and pear trees every winter. And if you prune the grapes before Christmas this year, you can make wreaths of the prunings for Christmas presents. The "bird house" gourds will make nice presents too and in the meantime they provide wonderful shade for the tool shed. It won't be long 'til Christmas, and that means fruit and seed catalogs will be coming in the mail. You can hardly wait to start planning for next year.

It took a little study and some careful thought and planning but much of it is just observation and experimentation. Some things work. Some things don't. It is always growing and changing. Just as you are.

"I know a bank where the wild thyme blows,
Where the oxlips and the nodding violet grows,
Quite over-canopied with luscious woodbine,
With sweet musk roses and with eglantine."

Shakespeare

"Earth laughs in flowers"
Emerson

Elderberry and Bird

First—A WORD ABOUT DIRT

This may seem a very BORING subject, but how you deal with your soil is the key to success or failure in all you do in your garden. Taking a few minutes now to learn how to build the kind of soil that will grow strong, vibrantly healthy plants, will save you a lot of frustration as well as time and money in the future. So I hope you will be motivated to take the time and effort needed to prepare your soil well. This bit is by far the toughest part of gardening and if you can't handle it yourself beg, borrow or hire someone who can! I can't stress this step enough. You may have the most wonderfully thought-out plan, and the highest quality plant material available, but if you plant in poor, under-nourished soil you are throwing your time and money away! The good news is, if you do the hard work right the first time you will only have to do it ONCE for the majority of your garden.

Healthy dirt is full of creepy-crawly things, from microscopic organisms and earthworms, to bugs and beetles. If you dig a hole and what you get is hard and compacted or looks a bit like beach sand, your dirt needs help. What it needs is ORGANIC MATTER—compost and aged manure*, "green manure", shredded leaves and other sorts of fluffy material, as well as a good helping of natural fertilizers like rock phosphate, greensand and bloodmeal. These will start biological activities going in your soil, turning the "stuff" you add into something plants can use. That organic matter will help create a soil texture that has air spaces and will hold moisture in a healthy way (not staying wet and soggy for days after a rain like heavy clay soil, or drying out in 15 minutes like a sandy soil can).

Growing "green manure" plants, like annual ryegrass, clover and buckwheat, and turning them into the soil is an inexpensive way to add organic matter to soil you haven't planted yet. Compost and well-aged manure can be spread around existing plantings and will be worked into the soil over time by all the critters that will have been encouraged to join the project.

Whatever you do, don't add chemical fertilizers to the soil, because they seem cheap and fast! They drive off and kill all the critters you need to encourage, and might well be why your soil is in the shape it is in to begin with!

***Fresh* manure can be too "hot" or potent and burn plants and roots.**

STEP BY STEP
Healthy Soil

The following guide will give you a "step by step" to achieving healthy, live soil. Happy digging!

1. Getting a soil test is an excellent start, although you can create great soil without it (your local Extension service can help you with the test).

2. Correct grade problems now: fill in low spots, add drainage where needed, etc.

3. Cultivate to a depth of 12 inches when soil is in a moist, crumbly state—not too *wet* (a clay soil that is too wet will compact and form clumps when tilled, and do more harm than good!).

4. Haul off any rocks, roots, weeds and debris you find.

5. Spread organic fertilizers according to soil test results (see the chart in Appendices).

6. Spread a 2"-6" layer of well-aged manure, compost or peat moss over the entire surface of the soil.

7. Rototill or otherwise mix well into soil.

8. If time permits, moisten soil well and allow it to sit for 1-2 weeks, in order to germinate any remaining weed seeds. Then cultivate again and rake out.

9. For vegetable gardens, now is the time to create "raised beds". (See the following special instructions.)

10. Now you can plant!

RAISED BED VEGETABLE GARDENING

In most of the northern half of the continent where spring is cool and accompanied by April showers, raised beds are a good alternative to the old row method because they warm up and dry out much earlier in spring than level ground and so can be planted earlier. Raised beds may be boxed with cedar or redwood or simply be flat-topped mounds. Four feet is a comfortable width for reaching from both sides and 15 feet or less a comfortable length. Anything longer and you will find yourself trying to step across them because of the distance around. These beds make much better use of the space available, using less for paths. The soil is always easy to work and with yearly additions of compost as mulch, should rarely need tilling. Since the soil is not walked on it never becomes compacted by foot traffic and because of the closer spacing possible for your plants, fewer weeds find space to grow. Protection from insects and cold with floating row covers is simplified as well.

In hot dry southern states these wide beds may be set in *trenches* of the same size, in order to cool soil and conserve moisture. Mulching heavily with compost is also a great help in moisture retention and cooling.

STEP BY STEP
Creating Raised Beds

1. Prepare the soil according to the directions in the previous section, using at least 2" of aged manure or compost.

2. If your soil is very heavy, incorporate a one to two inch layer of river sand into it during soil preparation.

3. Lay out your beds—4 feet by eight to fifteen feet is a comfortable size.

4. Rake loose soil from the pathways onto the bed areas. This will increase their height by 4"-6".

5. If you are going to build boxes for your beds, now is the time to do it. Don't use treated wood, as it will leach toxic chemicals into your soil and into your plants. Use 2" x 8" or 2" x 10" cedar, redwood or cypress.

6. Rake **flat** and level on top. Mounded beds are difficult to water evenly, as water tends to run off.

7. Spread a 1/2 inch layer of fine compost or bagged organic manure on top and rake in lightly. This will keep the surface from crusting.

8. Lay irrigation. "Ooze" soaker hose and drip lines may be laid down the center of each bed and buried 2"-3".

9. Plant seeds or plants.

RAISED BEDS

The second and following years:

FALL

1. Spread lime according to soil test to balance pH. Rake well into soil.

2. Seed empty beds with crimson clover, annual ryegrass, corn salad, fava beans or other winter cover crops.

3. Mulch overwintering crops with straw or leaves.

SPRING

1. Pull up clover, ryegrass, weeds, etc. or try turning under just enough clover to allow room for planting vegetable seeds or plants, and leave the rest as a living mulch.

2. In the fall, for a very early spring planting when the soil is still cool and wet, prepare bed with a covering of leaves or straw. Pull cover off in spring to plant.

3. Add a 1/2 inch layer of compost or manure and any fertilizers needed.

4. Rake amendments into the surface, preparing a smooth seed bed. Reshape the sides where needed, pulling loose soil up from paths.

5. Plant.

THE ILLUSIVE LOW-MAINTENANCE LAWN

Once upon a time a "flowery mead" was considered the ideal turf. Until the late 1950's a clover lawn was highly regarded and white dutch clover seed was a common part of every lawn seed mix. Then an enterprising grass seed and lawn chemical producer launched a campaign against clover and convinced us that it was a weed that didn't belong in a lawn.

Today there is a growing demand for "low-maintenance" lawns, inspired in part, I am sure, by the feeling that the green expanses of lawn that surround our homes take more from the environment, our pocketbook and our "free" time than they return. Just what is a low-maintenance lawn? The answer would depend, to a great extent, on the amount of care you are currently giving your lawn. Those who never water, fertilize or weed their lawns and only mow in the spring and fall when rains keep the grass growing, already have a low maintenance lawn. But for those who enjoy a lush green turf to lie on and play on all summer, the question is a serious one. It may, at this point in time, involve a change in attitude toward what constitutes a perfect lawn. If we let go of the demand for a golf course look-alike it is possible to have a healthy, green lawn that needs watering only 3-5 times a year, mowing once every 3-4 weeks during the growing season and requires no fertilizer or pesticides. The trade off? This lawn has flowers! It is a combination of low-growing grasses, English lawn daisies, yarrow, chamomile and strawberry clover (there are few bee problems with this clover). This mix creates a lovely dark green lawn that changes over the growing season as the various plants come into bloom. The clippings are left unless they are very long (then they are bagged and composted). All the fertilizer necessary is supplied naturally by the strawberry clover and the clippings. Pesticides have not been needed on these lawns.

Tom Cook, Associate Professor of Horticulture at Oregon State University, has maintained test plots of several mixes with 1½" of water applied once a month during the dry summer months. They are mowed to 2" every 3 weeks with the clippings left on the lawn. No fertilizers or pesticides have been used. The mix that works best with this low maintenance schedule includes perennial ryegrass and Kentucky bluegrass. This mix is sold by Hobbs & Hopkins (see appendix) under the name of Fleur de Lawn. These grasses do not crowd out the flowers as hard fescue, chewings fescue and bentgrass do (once these grasses take over a plot they become clumpy and weedy). The broadleaf flowering plants are important to the mix because of their ability to stay green in low maintenance situations. The grasses will normally become dormant between watering, with the broadleaf flowering plants masking them, maintaining the uniform green look.

Only a few miles from the OSU test plots, Rosemarie McGee of Nichols Garden Nursery (see appendix) has maintained a plot of Ecology Lawn for 9 years. This lawn consists of the same flower mix with creeping bentgrass instead of ryegrass and bluegrass. Her plot is not watered on a schedule, but only when it begins to look stressed (about every 3-5 weeks in summer). It is not mowed as regularly either, and if the clippings are too long to leave, they are bagged and composted (this can happen in a long wet spring when mowing on a schedule is difficult). This lawn receives a much less scientific, more relaxed treatment—has never been fertilized or had pesticides used on it, and yet has maintained a stable mix of flowers and grass for nine years. Creeping bentgrass is normally thought of as a high maintenance, high-water-user (it is used for golf courses), so the success of the plot at Nichols Nursery is all the more interesting. The experience at both these sites would vary in different parts of the country. *Some* water was important to both these plots. The flowering plants are unable to survive with *no* summer water.

Other plants that could be included in a flowering lawn are violets (for shady lawns), veronica (speedwell), oxalis and sweet alyssum. In fact the possibilities are endless! A mix of just yarrow and hard fescue is showing a lot of promise at the OSU test plots. The yarrow is dark green and feathery, wears well and is very drought tolerant. It rarely flowers with this kind of mowing cycle, but maintains a soft dark green lawn that needs very little water.

Buffalo Grass has been much touted as a drought resistant alternative, but has serious drawbacks for the lawn lover. It not only turns brown in mid-summer but again in the fall when it goes dormant for the winter. Dwarf alpine grasses are currently being tested in Canada, but it is possible that under *non*-alpine situations these may lose the very qualities they were chosen for, as in the case of dwarfed trees brought from their mountainous homes to milder low-altitude sites.

Hobbs & Hopkins sells a mix called Companion Grass that was developed for orchards and vineyards. It is a combination of Elka ryegrass and Ensylva creeping red fescue and grows slowly to 12-14" if uncut and unwatered. (These grasses cannot survive a drought without *any* water, however.) It may also be a good choice in a meadow mix.

Many grasses are being developed for their drought-tolerance and drought-resistance (in the one instance a plant maintains its good looks with little water, in the other it goes dormant and brown, but *survives*), and for their slow-growing qualities. A new vision of the perfect lawn that includes flowers in the picture may be our quickest route to the illusive low maintenance lawn for now. With all the work being done in the field new strategies come along every day. So stay tuned!

OVERSEEDING AN EXISTING LAWN

If your lawn is badly compacted and absorbs water poorly, it may be best to till in 2"-3" of organic matter and *start over* (see Steps to Healthy Soil in Chapter 2). Otherwise you may try mowing closely, de-thatching (with a rented machine) seeding with either the Ecology Lawn Mix from Nichols (flowers and Bentgrass), Hobbs & Hopkins' Fluer de Lawn (flowers and ryegrass) or a mix you have developed yourself. The best times to plant are spring or early fall. If you choose to mulch the seed, do so *lightly,* as many of the flower seeds are very small.

Fertilizer is usually not needed unless your soil tests especially low in phosphorus or potassium. Any addition of nitrogen would encourage growth of the **grasses** at the expense of the broadleaf flowering plants. What makes these mixes work as a low maintenance lawn is the ability of the flowering plants to stay green when the grasses go dormant—so a good balance of grass and flowers is needed.

COMPOST—A GARDENER'S BEST FRIEND

Compost piles have a reputation in some quarters for being smelly and attracting flies. That's only because many well-meaning people have built them without understanding how to do it right. And doing it right is no *harder*, only different!

If you want to avoid a smelly pile that draws flies, and your neighbors disapproving glare, don't ever add meat scraps or dairy products to it. Also, never throw the already decomposing leftovers from Saturdays frig clean-out on **top** of your pile, bury the leftovers in the center of the pile. Get rid of the meat scraps and dairy leftovers some other way (the neighbors dog?). An alternative for kitchen scraps is a WORM BIN on the back porch. Worms make undemanding "pets" who will live on what you throw away, and in return, create some rich compost!

The trick with compost is to have a good balance of wet "green" material and dry "brown" material to keep it fluffy enough to allow air through the pile. It is important to keep it from being soggy and matted down. Keep a bale of straw or a pile of last fall's leaves next to the bin so you have some brown fluffy stuff to toss on top of each layer of wet greens you put in. Keep the pile *slightly* moist all the time. Running a hose on it now and then during dry weather works, then throw a plastic tarp on it during the wet part of the year.

The thing is, even if you don't do it any special way and simply toss it all in an unlovely heap in the back corner of the yard (but *do* bury the kitchen scraps or put them in a worm bin) after a year or two, most of it will be compost anyway. With a little attention it works much faster (turning it every two weeks works wonders!). Once you see how great compost is and the many ways you can use it, you'll wish you had truckloads of it, and may even start combing the neighborhood for more materials to add to it. A word of caution here: if your neighbor uses chemicals in the form of "weed and feed" or pesticides on his lawn or herbicides on his weeds, they can transfer to your soil and plants. So you might ask first.

Compost made from a variety of materials is highly nutritious. When applied regularly to soil, you may need no additional fertilizer, and it can be used for seed sowing, potting mixes, lawn top-dressing and plant mulch.

COMPOST GUIDELINES

✦ **Use old compost or healthy soil as a "starter".** The micro-organisms in these will get the decomposition process going. Mix "browns" and "greens" together when your bin is full, for a faster, more consistent compost. After this mix, little or no turning is needed. Simply maintain a slightly moist pile and you'll get great compost with no additional work.

✦ **Grass clippings are better left on the lawn** where they will act as fertilizer. If they are too long to do this without matting, allow them to dry out a bit in the sun. Then compost them or use them as a thin mulch around veggies.

✦ **Shredded or chopped materials decompose faster.** Try running a mower over your pile of weeds or leaves. A shredder/grinder is even better!

✦ **Things to use:** Vegetable and fruit waste, hay, sod, weeds and leaves.

✦ **Things to keep out:** Meat and dairy products, noxious weeds such as bindweed, poison oak, poison ivy, and quackgrass; pet waste. Avoid diseased plants as it takes a very hot pile to kill the disease pathogens.

✦ **Finished compost will smell like rich earth and be fluffy and crumbly.**

SOME COMPOSTING IDEAS

❧ Any unfinished compost remaining in the spring can be spread thickly—6 inches or more—in an area you wish to improve, and then planted with potatoes, pumpkins or winter squash. By harvest time you will have a bed of fine finished compost and a much improved soil underneath.

❧ Ready-made bins are available, but they can be easily made from such things as stacked concrete blocks, picket, wire or snow fencing, or 36 inch "hardware cloth" formed into a large ring. (Any structure that will retain composting material and allow some air circulation.)

❧ BAG COMPOSTING is easy, too. Plant wastes and bagged chicken manure or organic fertilizers are mixed well together in a large plastic yard bag, moistened lightly, tied up and set aside for 2-3 months.

❧ Another excellent method of composting is a WORM BIN. A simple tidy bin can be made from a large covered plastic storage box with small holes poked in the top and upper sides. It should be 8"-24" deep and 24"x24" or 24"x36" for larger families. Fill it nearly to the top with **shredded** newspaper (black and white only), computer paper, cardboard or any *uncolored* paper then moisten well (not wet) and put one pound of Red Wigglers or Red Manure worms on top. Keep a small bucket under the sink for kitchen scraps and every few days dig a *new* hole in the worm bedding and bury the buckets contents. Keep the bin in a handy place that won't freeze in winter or bake in summer. Renew two thirds of the bedding every 2-3 months and toss the finished compost on your garden or tuck around your house-plants. For more detailed instructions read *"Worms Eat My Garbage"* by Mary Appelhof.

GROW YOUR OWN FERTILIZERS
Green manures and cover crops

"Green manure" is a cover crop that is turned into the soil and allowed to decompose. Green manures have long been used by wise farmers to improve their soil. Now home gardeners are discovering the advantages to even very small areas. They reduce weeds and hold nutrients in the soil over winter that might be leached away by rains. Their root systems bring nutrients up where they can be used by crops and when they are turned into the soil they enhance biological activity, increase the organic content, add humus and improve the tilth and structure of the soil. And last but certainly not least, some provide spectacular bloom.

* **NITROGEN**—Legumes (lupine, clovers, alfalfa, peas, beans, vetch). Till these under *before they bloom*, for the best supply of nitrogen.

* **PHOSPHORUS**—Alfalfa, mustard, buckwheat.

* **POTASSIUM**—Vetches.

* **BENEFICIAL INSECT FOOD**—Buckwheat, alfalfa, white dutch clover, white mustard.

* **WINTER COVER**—fava beans, winter rye, scotch kale.

* **SOIL LOOSENER FOR HEAVY SOILS**—Mustard, buckwheat, alfalfa (these three are good for all sorts of things!).

* **SPECTACULAR BLOOM**—Crimson clover, birdsfoot trefoil, lupine, mustard and sunflower.

The Grape Arbor and the Children's Garden

Edibles in Your Garden

Chestnuts, Chickweed, Cherries and Corn

Having lots of tasty things to eat growing in your yard is great, but your life is so full you haven't much time or energy to devote to it all. So you have limited those things that demand relatively high attention to a few special plants and areas. Like the very special dwarf apple and pear trees espaliered near the garden, and the seedless grape vine over the children's play area. The grape grows on an arbor, from which a swing and a climbing rope hang. It shades the sand box and will one day shade a hammock. Back near the chicken house raspberries grow supported by posts and wire to keep them neat and easy to reach. Along with your kitchen garden these demand the most of you, but they are special to you and your family and are worth the little extra effort involved. The kitchen garden is near the back door and has been designed for easy maintenance. The soil is rich and deep and soft from yearly additions of compost and only needs to be raked out before planting. Little weeding is needed here and the odd purslane, lamb's quarters and chickweed volunteers (usually thought of as "weeds") are harvested and enjoyed along with lettuce and French sorrel in salads. Nasturtiums, California poppy, sweet alyssum and calendula pop up serendipitously here and there each year, and you always enjoy the cheerful effect they have on the garden. Extras are moved to bare spots around the yard or added to the compost. For the remainder of the yard you have chosen edibles that demand little attention except at harvest time, and those that will feed other creatures too.

The dainty musk strawberries that grow in your woodland garden are the first fruit of the season. You have given them space to wander under the Cornelian cherry, with its golden mist of spring flowers. The bright red fruit of this dogwood relative has been a European favorite for hundreds of years. The fruit you haven't eaten right off the tree in late summer, you turn into syrup or freeze. The birds love it too, as they do the juneberry, the next fruit to ripen in the garden. It's sweet, juicy berries must be harvested quickly or the birds take them all! The juneberry shares the dappled woodland under the tall oaks and sugar maples with the Cornelian cherry and a pair of native American pawpaw trees. The pawpaw's fat banana-like fruit isn't ripe till late summer. Right now you enjoy the big pink flowers that smell like ripening grapes. None of these trees need pruning or spraying, so their fruit is a delightful gift!

Scattered along the path that winds through these trees you have planted several Pacific Northwest natives—the Oregon grape, salal and evergreen huckleberry. All bear small tart, edible berries. Carpeting the woodland floor in loose wandering drifts among the ferns and wildflowers are lingonberries and sweet woodruff, with its dainty white flowers and fragrant foliage. At the edge of the woodland bordering your mowed meadow path, where the sunshine hits in the afternoon, the ground is covered by dwarf blueberries. Their fiery red, autumn leaves light up the woodland floor.

In a low damp area near your lily pond grows a little quince tree, whose fragrant yellow fruit adds sparkle to your jellies. The low evergreen cranberries and wintergreen growing beneath the tree thrive in the damp soil there and add to the bounty of food and beauty. The kids love the wintergreen syrup you make for sore throats, and you enjoy the berries in tea.

Across the front of your property you and your family planted what the kids call the "vitamin C" hedge! This tall, colorful hedge is made up of Highbush cranberry, Nanking cherry, Rugosa rose and black currant bushes and only needs occasional thinning to keep it doing well (nearly all the fruit is especially high in vitamin C). Again, the birds and other critters love the fruit as much as you do, but there is always enough to go around.

Nearby grows an American persimmon tree, shading the house from the late afternoon sun. In the carpet of white dutch clover at its base, you have naturalized daffodils. After the daffodils die back in early summer you mow the clover and add the cuttings to your compost. In the fall the persimmon's leaves turn gold and crimson and when they drop the bare branches are left decorated by the big red fruit looking for all the world like Christmas ornaments.

The Chinese chestnuts you planted for shade along the drive 5 years ago are not only becoming magnificent trees but are already supplying your family with enough nuts to last the winter. Those you don't use at Thanksgiving and Christmas are frozen for roasting on long winter evenings or left to feed the squirrels and other critters. The only work you do for these is mowing the birdsfoot trefoil that covers the ground beneath in time for the nuts to fall and be gathered. The trefoil is covered with yellow flowers most of the summer and will someday be shaded out as the trees grow, then sweet woodruff will be planted in its place.

Your favorite spot for morning tea is under the elderberry near the shed. Every three or four years it gets cut to the ground (called "stooling") and comes back up new and fresh. Otherwise it needs no help from you to produce its many clusters of tiny blue berries each year! In its shade grow a slowly expanding mass of daylilies. Each flower lasts only a day and you often pick the still fresh blossoms in the evening to add their delicate flavor to a salad. In front of the shed grows a border of alpine strawberries, a dainty non-spreading strawberry that bears small exquisitely sweet fruit all summer long. Everyone loves these and there never seem to be enough! Thank goodness for all the other tasty fruits to graze on, those lazy summer afternoons!

On the near edge of the meadow you maintain a wide strip of ground where you rotate patches of corn, potatoes, drying beans, winter squash, a "green manure" crop and a patch you plant just for the birds and other small creatures. Here you plant a merry mix of sunflowers, deep red amaranth, millet, wheat and oats. Each fall some seed is saved to replant in the spring and the rest is left as winter wildlife food. The "green manure" crop is chopped into the soil in the fall and planted in a different section each year for six years, rotating with the other veggies. This keeps the soil healthy and alive and along with the yearly layer of compost nothing more is needed. At the end of this strip is a permanent bed of Jerusalem artichokes, their tall yellow daisy flowers swaying in the autumn sunshine. They add a friendly touch to the meadow's edge giving no hint of the sweet lumpy tubers beneath their feet. The ground here is covered with straw each fall to make harvesting the roots easier all winter. The kitchen garden is covered with a snug blanket of straw as well, pulled up close to the overwintering vegetables growing there in late fall. Most of the hay will be taken off in early spring to allow the soil to warm and dry, getting ready for next season's plants.

In March you keep a pot of maple and birch sap simmering on the wood stove, adding to it every couple of days from the pots hung on your woodland trees. You only end up with a few pints of syrup each year to share with friends and trade for some of your neighbor's honey, but what a treat!

It all took time and energy—planning, planting and caring for it all until it got established and filled in. Each year it demands less and adds more to your life as well as the lives of all the other creatures living here. A truly wonderful arrangement!

Filbert

"The bees rove and revel,
rejoicing in the bounty of the sun,
clambering eagerly through bramble and hucklebloom,
ringing the myriad bells of the manzanita,
now humming aloft among polleny willow and firs,
now...plunging deep into snowy banks of cherry and buckthorn."

John Muir, "The Mountains of California"

EDIBLES

Nurseries across the country are becoming aware of the increasing desire to grow a broad range of low-care edibles, not just for ourselves but for birds and other wild creatures, and they are making these more available to the home gardener.

Although I concentrate here on the more uncommon fruits, don't feel I am discouraging the use of the more common ones. If you do choose to grow apples, pears, raspberries, etc. look for *varieties* of these plants that are especially flavorful and insect and disease resistant.

The fruits and nuts mentioned here are a very small sampling of those that could be grown by the home gardener. There is such a wide range of food bearing plant material for every climate and every purpose that no space need be without one or two.

GOURMET FRUITS

CORNUS MAS—*The Cornelian Cherry* or cherry dogwood   Zones 1-6

This small (20-25'), hardy, deciduous forest tree is self-fertile with fruit that ripens in late summer through fall. It has a very hard wood that is highly regarded in Europe and used for making musical instruments and furniture. The fruit was enjoyed by the Romans and Greeks 2000 years ago, but the tree is used primarily as an ornamental in North America. It is a long-lived tree (200 year old trees are still bearing fruit in Europe) and its bright red fruit have a plum/berry/cherry flavor. The tiny yellow flowers are borne very early in spring, in such profusion that the tree appears in a yellow mist. In fall the leaves may turn deep red. It does well in shade, although it bears more heavily in sun, and needs little or no pruning or spraying. Birds will compete for the sweet fruit, which the Europeans turn into syrup, juice, wine, conserves and tarts. They are good fresh, canned or frozen. The fruit, leaves and bark all are known to have many fine medicinal qualities.

CYDONIA—*The Fruiting Quince*   All zones

This small deciduous tree grows slowly to 10-20 feet and is one of the lovelier fruiting trees available to the home gardener. It has large white to pink flowers in spring and its leaves turn yellow in the fall. In winter its gnarled twisted branches form dramatic patterns. It tolerates heavy wet soil and needs little pruning or fertilizing.

The fragrant yellow fruit is not eaten raw but is delicious stewed, baked or made into preserves and jellies, and is high in calcium, phosphorus, potassium and iron. When ripe it can be stored for 2 months or more.

RUBUS—*Thornless Erect Blackberry "Navaho"*   All zones

A very hardy (to minus 9 degrees!) self-supporting blackberry needing no trellising to keep it neat. It is sweeter than other varieties of blackberry and its fine appearance and delicious flavor make it a valuable home garden plant.

FEIJOA SELLOWIANA—*Pineapple Guava*   Zones 7-9 and 12-24

A lovely, large evergreen shrub, that can grow to 20 feet if not killed back by frost and is easy to espalier or use as a hedge. It bears bright pink and red edible flowers with the flavor of cotton candy! It is a drought-tolerant and insect and disease-free plant, and given a protected sunny spot in northern areas and a little shade in hotter climates, it will bear its dark green fruit reliably with little attention. The fruit has a minty-pineapple flavor as the name implies, and it ripens mid-November to December in northern areas. It needs a pollinator—any 2 varieties will do. A shrub worthy of a little special attention!

FRAGARIA VESCA & FRAGARIA MOSCHATA
Alpine and Musk Strawberries   Zones 3-10

These near-wild strawberries are self-pollinators, the alpine bearing spring to fall and the musk fruiting only in spring. They are not nearly as productive as cultivated berries, but the small, sweet berries are wonderfully delectable and considered a delicacy in Europe. Both need only 4 hours of sun, but must have a rich, humusy, moisture-retentive soil (like a forest floor!). An organic mulch is important to protect the shallow roots.

The alpine is a dainty plant from the Alps in France that does not send out runners, so it makes an ideal edging plant. The musk strawberry is a larger plant that is found wild in European forests and can be used as an edible **groundcover** because it *does* put out runners.

HOVENIA DULCIS—*The Raisin Tree*　　　　Zones 3-9 and 13-24

This small (20-30') hardy, deciduous tree is easy to grow and adaptable to many soils. A quietly beautiful tree, with large glossy heart-shaped leaves, it is good for moist, shady areas, although it bears more fruit in full sun. It produces masses of fragrant purple or cream flowers in late June or early July and the edible fruit stalk, called a penduncle, ripens late in fall. The Chinese have enjoyed them since before the time of Confucius. It has virtually no pest problems in North America, and needs no pollinator. It makes an attractive shade tree for a small garden.

MESPILUS GERMANICA—*The Persian Medlar*　　　　Zones 1-6

The Medlar is a beautiful 20 foot, flat-topped tree with contorting branches. A profusion of 2" white to pink wild rose-like flowers cover the tree in late spring followed by 2" crabapple shaped fruit, with a flavor resembling cinnamon-flavored applesauce. The fruit is best harvested in fall after leaf-drop and allowed to soften indoors. Can be stored calyx side down, on a shelf for several weeks, and used for jelly, jam, drinks, mousse and syrup.

PUNICA GRANATUM—*Pomegranate*　　　　Zones 7-24; 5
and 6 if against a　south or west facing wall.

This self-fertile shrub or small tree is deciduous and grows to a possible 12'. It is hardy to only 12 degrees, but will regrow from roots at colder temperatures. A showy, easy to grow plant, its beautiful orange red flowers will be enjoyed even in climates where the bright red fruit doesn't ripen. It needs sun for the best fruit but needs little water once established, although regular water produces the best fruit. "Sweet" and "Wonderful" are good fruiting varieties. The leaves turn bright yellow in fall.

PRUNUS TOMENTOSA—*The Nanking Cherry*

All Zones

Grown as a small tree or large shrub, a hedge, or a windbreak, this self-fertile cherry is beautiful in all seasons, with lustrous orange-brown bark in winter, profuse early white spring flowers followed by abundant red fruit in mid-summer. It is drought-tolerant if not grown from cuttings, will grow almost anywhere, and may need no pest control although it is sometimes subject to the usual "prunus" pests. The fruit is delicious right off the bush!

PYRUS PYRIFOLIA—*The Asian Pear*

Zones 1-9 and 14-24

A very hardy, long-lived tree that can reach 50' in 100 years or so, but is more often seen at 25'-30'. Many plants are now sold on dwarfing stock that will allow you to maintain a tree from 8'-15'. This popular oriental fruit has been grown for 3000 years in China, where there are several thousand cultivars available. The tree bears better fruit with cross pollination and the early blooming varieties of European pears can be used for this. The sweet crispness of this apple-shaped fruit is very different from the common pear and juicier than an apple, and should be allowed to ripen on the tree. It is a lovely ornamental tree.

RIBES UVA-CRISPA—*The European Gooseberry*

Zones 1-6 and 17

Grow this 3'-5' self-fertile deciduous shrub in dappled shade, with good air circulation to avoid mildew problems, and it will reward you with fruit through-out the summer. A good cultivar will bear large luscious fruit with a tender skin and sweet aromatic pulp as good as any grape or apple. It is cold hardy and likes cool, moist summers. The European and American crosses are best, "Poorman" and "Colossal" are good varieties. It is a thorny plant and because of its pruning needs wouldn't make a good hedge.

ROSA RUGOSA—*The Rose Hip Rose*   All Zones

Wonderful, disease-resistant shrub roses, extremely easy to grow, and fine deciduous hedge plants, growing to 6 feet tall. They are very hardy and many fragrant varieties bloom all season long, becoming decorated in summer and fall with huge rose "hips". These are one of the finest sources of vitamin C and can be eaten fresh or dried and ground into powder and used in anything and everything!

ZIZIPHUS JUJUBA—*'Jujube'* or Chinese date   Zones 7-16 and 18-24

The Chinese have been growing and eating the fruit of this small (30') tree for 4000 years. It is deciduous, self-fertile and hardy to minus 20 degrees and adaptable to a wide range of soils and moisture conditions. It is extremely drought-tolerant and has no pest problems. It does well in desert conditions but prefers regular garden soil and water. It likes being planted in a lawn.

The jujube is a graceful narrow tree usually grown in the U.S. as an ornamental, with small yellow flowers appearing throughout the season on naturally drooping branches. The 1-2" fruit is dark red and shiny when ripe and resembles a date in appearance, texture and taste, although at the beginning of the ripening process they are crisply sweet like an apple. It ripens over a month or so, but may be picked under-ripe and ripened indoors and will keep 1-2 months at 50 degrees. Dried fruits keep up to a year if kept cool.

NATIVE FRUITS

AMELANCHIER—*Juneberry, Serviceberry or Sarviceberry*   All zones

This handsome native grows anywhere in the U.S. and Canada and was eaten with game by Native Americans. It is self-fertile and deciduous and grows as a small tree or large shrub. The blueberry-sized fruit is usually blue or purple although some plants bear red or even white fruit. They are juicy and sweet and you will need to be quick to beat the birds to them. The trees are easy to care for and only need occasional pruning if grown as a tree. If grown as a shrub or hedge plant you will get the best fruit by pruning out the old wood each winter. It does well in sun or part shade, and its white spring flowers and purple, orange and yellow fall leaves would make it a decorative addition to a woodland garden, even if it had no fruit.

ASIMINA TRILOBA—*Pawpaw Tree* All zones

This 10'-25' deciduous tree is native to Eastern U.S. woodlands and is easy to grow in a wide range of climates. It is hardy to minus 30 degrees. It will need no pruning or spraying, but will need a pollinator. The 2" flowers turn from pink to purple and each can produce several fruit. The flowers have the fragrance of ripening grapes, and the 3"-6" fruit looks like a fat banana. The custardy flesh has a hint of pineapple, mango and vanilla custard. Mulch the ground under the tree thickly in the late summer and fall, to cushion the falling fruit, which are best eaten after they have fallen from the tree. Firm fruit may be picked and will store for several months, or the pulp may be dried. Native Americans enjoyed the fruit and used the soft inner bark to weave cloth.

CRATAEGUS AESTEVALES—*The Mayhaw Tree* Zones 1-11

This southern edible Hawthorn (**May** blooming **Haw**thorn) is deciduous and grows to 25'. The red to yellow fruit (depending on type) ripens in early fall. The fruit is 1/3" to 2/3" across, tastes like a tart crabapple and is good for juice, jelly and preserves. The tree is broad-topped and thorny and is attractive with its cloud of white to pink blossoms in early spring. It likes well-drained, slightly acid soil but will survive in boggy areas by ponds and rivers. Plant two trees for cross pollination. Planted in zones 6-9 it is hardy to minus 15 degrees but will most likely not fruit at colder temperatures.

DIOSPYROS VIRGINIANA—*American Persimmon Tree*   Zones 2-9 and 14-16

Millions of Orientals eat persimmons and so did Native Americans, who removed the seed and dried the pulp, adding it to corn cake. The early settlers made fruit butter with the dried pulp and honey. The ripe fruit has a soft rich flavor but the un-ripe fruit is astringent.

While the American persimmon is occasionally self-fertile, it will produce better crops with a male tree for pollination. It is an especially beautiful, deciduous ornamental, and grows to 30' in height. Persimmons are easy to care for, need no pruning, and are pest and disease-free, as well as drought-tolerant! In the fall the leaves turn gold and scarlet and after they fall the tree is left decorated by the bright orange fruit for a month or more, which can even be picked frozen! Purchase as young trees because the long tap root makes transplanting difficult when the tree is older. A great addition to any landscape!

MORUS ALBA, RUBRA, AND NIGRA—*Mulberry Tree*
All zones (Nigra—zones 7-24)

This large deciduous tree is self-fertile and its blackberry shaped fruit ripens over a long period in summer. They are a very sweet fruit, often too sweet for adults taste, but loved by children everywhere. The Russian variety is very drought-resistant and makes a good fruiting hedge. Its fruit can be dried like raisins. The Illinois Everbearing is a smaller tree, growing to 35' or less, and its fruit has a touch of tartness that is preferred by adults. It is hardy to minus 30 degrees and bears all summer. It needs no pruning and has few disease or pest problems. Don't plant it where falling fruit can stain sidewalks, patios or play areas and expect the birds to delight in it as much as you do (it has been said that birds will leave other fruit alone as long as there are mulberries to eat).

PASSIFLORA INCARNATA—*Maypop Vine* or Northern Passionflower   All zones

This deciduous perennial vine needs a pollinator to produce its late summer fruit. It is a cold-hardy relative of the tropical passionflower, and although some wild fruit may not be as tasty as the fruit of this southern vine, the fruit of the cultivated northern plant is every bit as good. The vine clings by tendrils and dies to the ground each year. It doesn't begin new growth until early summer (so don't panic and think it died!) but then it takes off, and may quickly grow to 20'. It blooms from July to frost and its huge fragrant lavender, white and purple flowers last only one day. The vine will grow in full sun or partial shade but you will get less fruit in the shade. In very cold areas it can be grown on a sunny south wall and mulched well in winter. Train it over an early flowering shrub like a lilac or on a chain link fence or simply trellis it. The delicately delicious fruit may be eaten fresh or used in juice.

RIBES NIGRUM—*Black Currant*   Best in zones 1-6 and 17-Grown in all zones

The Black Currant is a mostly self-fertile deciduous shrub that grows to 3' to 6' and makes an attractive addition to a fruiting hedge. Its small tasty black berries ripen mid to late summer and are high in vitamin C. They make a syrup that is good for sore throats and are delicious in tarts or as wine, juice, jam or jelly. It does well in sun or part shade and should have the oldest branches pruned out occasionally.

SAMBUCUS CANADENSIS—*Elderberry*   Zones 1-17

Both the eastern purple-fruited and the west coast blue-fruited native elderberry are small deciduous trees that are improved by occasional "stooling" (cutting to the ground in early spring). They will quickly grow to their usual 10'-15' height in one season and produce a better crop of berries for it! The wood is prized for musical instruments and the leaves work as a mosquito repellent when rubbed on the clothing. A blend of the tiny white flowers with five parts water is thought to be a good repellent for aphids. But, above all, these little berries, which are a good source of vitamin C, are valued for the jelly, sauce, wine and syrup they make. An easy care plant. "Nova" is an especially high yield variety and is available through Bear Creek Nursery (see Source list in Appendices).

VACCINUM OVATUM—*Evergreen Huckleberry*   Zones 4-7 and 14-17

A beautiful evergreen shrub with a touch of red in the new leaves, this Northwest native will grow to 8' in the shade and 4' in full sun. It is hardy to zone 6 and is an easy plant to care for, having no disease or pest problems and needing no pruning to keep it looking good. It would make a lovely evergreen hedge. The small pinkish flowers are followed in summer by delicious and slightly tart black berries that make wonderful pies, pancakes, muffins and syrups.

VIBURNUM TRILOBUM—*Highbush Cranberry*   All zones

This tall hardy deciduous shrub is more often grown for its looks than its tasty red fruit. It is lovely in bloom and its leaves turn fiery red in fall before they drop. It is easy to grow, demanding little of its caretaker, and will grow happily in the shade. The fruit, which is high in vitamin C, makes good syrup, preserves or wine. This is a great addition to a fruit hedge or grown on its own. There is a dwarf variety available now, too.

GROUNDCOVER EDIBLES

GAULTHERIA PROCUMBENS—*Wintergreen*   Zones 1-7 and 14-17

A relative of the west coast native salal, which also makes a nice evergreen edible groundcover, wintergreen is useful in woodland gardens, rockeries, and shrub borders. It likes an acid, peaty soil like that found on the forest floor and will tolerate a fairly wet soil. The bright red fruit is highly flavored as are the leaves and both make an excellent tea that is known to reduce fever. It grows only 6" tall and spreads by underground runners. It is a lovely non-aggressive addition to a woodland.

VACCINUM ANGUSTIFOLIUM—*Lowbush Blueberry*   Zones 1-9

These low-growing blueberries are deciduous shrubs native to the eastern U.S. Their mid-summer fruit is sweeter than the more common highbush blueberry. Very hardy (to minus 35 degrees) they are easy to care for and grow to 10"-24". They do well with a hard pruning (to 2" tall) every 3-4 years and like a thick mulch of sawdust or leaves each year. They make a beautiful groundcover or border plant and in fall turn a brilliant crimson!

VACCINUM CRASSIFOLIUM—*Creeping Blueberry*   Zones 4-9

A creeping evergreen blueberry! What next? This evergreen is native to the East Coast of the U.S. and is grown much like its relatives in an acid soil in sun to part shade. It is not as hardy as most but will survive brief low temperatures. "Bloodstone" has red stems and leaves and "Wells Delight" is a ground hugger with small dark green leaves. These are available at Woodlanders, 1128 Colleton Ave., Aiken, S.C. 29801

VACCINUM MACROCARPA—*Creeping Cranberry*   Zones 2-7 and 14-17

Another *Vaccinum* that grows as a groundcover, this is the traditional Thanksgiving cranberry. It is a fast spreader and a very productive fruiter. It is evergreen as well, bears small pink flowers in spring, and grows only a few inches tall. It actually prefers a moist soil so if you have a boggy area where nothing seems to grow, try this. It needs full sun, unlike most of its relatives.

VACCINUM VITIS-IDEA—*Lingonberry*   Zones 2-7 and 14-17

This dainty evergreen groundcover is a good companion to Rhododendrons in a woodland garden as it loves shade and an acid soil. It grows to 12" or so and spreads slowly by underground runners, never making a pest of itself. The flowers are white or pinkish bells and appear in May followed by edible red berries like tiny cranberries. They are highly prized for preserves and syrup.

CLIMBING EDIBLES

AKEBIA All zones—Evergreen in milder climates.

A hardy fast growing vine needing a pollinator. Its deep pink fragrant flowers are followed by strange sausage shaped fruit with a tough inedible skin. The pulp inside however is edible and sweet. The vine is semi-evergreen and hardy throughout most of the U.S. It can spread up to 20', and benefits from an annual pruning. It is a lovely vine that can even be grown in partial shade.

ACTINIDIA DELICIOSA, A. ARGUTA and A. KOLOMITKA
The Kiwi Vine Zones 4-6 and 14-24

These natives to the humid mountain forests of eastern Asia have finally made it to American gardens! They are all large deciduous woody vines that need a male pollinator (with 1 or 2 exceptions), and grow best in well drained soil. North facing slopes and sites shielded from low winter and early spring sun are best, to keep them from blooming too early. All are high in vitamin C.

Deliciosa is the well-known kiwi fruit made popular by New Zealand growers and it is hardy in zones 7-9 . It is a large vine that needs both male and female vines to bear fruit and has big thick fuzzy leaves.

Arguta is the Hardy kiwi and is good for zones 4-7. It is a vigorous ornamental vine with a more delicate appearance than *Deliciosa* and the fruit is said to be sweeter. The leaves and fruit are not fuzzy and the grape-sized fruit is borne in clusters.

Kolomikta is called the 'Arctic Beauty' and hardy in the much lower temperatures of zone 3. This vine likes a bit of shade so is useful to the gardener with limited sun. It is also less rampant than its relatives and extremely decorative, bearing white and pink variegated leaves primarily on the male vines. Outside of the pruning requirements these are all easy vines to grow, having no insect or disease problems.

Also see *Maypop* under NATIVE FRUITS.

ESPECIALLY GOOD NUT TREES

CASTANEA MOLLISSIMA—*Chinese Chestnut* Zones 1-9 and 14-17

This beautiful ornamental shade tree is hardy to minus 25 degrees and is an easy tree to grow. It is not plagued by the blight that all but wiped out the American chestnut. Creamy white catkins bloom in June and July and the nuts are enclosed in a prickly bur. It grows to 60' and begins to bear nuts only 2-3 years after planting. You will need two trees for cross-pollination. The nuts can be frozen and used until the next crop comes on.

CORYLUS MAXIMA or AVELLANA or AMERICANA—*Filbert*
Zones 1-9 and 14-20

Another good landscaping tree, which also needs a pollinator, its long yellow catkins are lovely in winter. *Americana* is native to much of the U.S. and *Avellana* is good primarily in the Pacific Northwest. This tree makes a good hedgerow and windbreak and can be kept pruned to 12' or allowed to grow slowly to 20'. This is an easy-to-grow tree, featuring nuts that are easy-to-harvest and crack, and are high in nutrition.

JUGLANS REGIA—*Walnut (Persian or English)* Zones 4-9 and 13-23

This tree is self-fertile making it a good choice as a single large shade tree to 40' or more. It is a magnificent tree requiring little care once it is established. Everyone is familiar with the wonderful nuts, which are highly nutritious, fairly easy to harvest and store for many months. A very special tree!

CARYA ILLINOINENSIS—*Pecan* Zones 7-9, 12-16 and 18-23

This self-fertile native of the southern and central U.S. is a large shapely deciduous tree to 70' tall. It is a good ornamental shade tree that needs little pruning and is easy to care for. Give this deeply rooted tree, deep well-drained soil and mulch with aged manure. Select varieties suited to your particular climate. The nuts are a rich source of vegetable proteins, phosphorus, vitamin B1, calcium and iron.

MINI-FRUIT TREES

True dwarf trees (as opposed to trees grafted onto dwarfing rootstocks) rarely reach more than 6 feet. Those available to the home gardener now are Peach, Nectarine, Cherry, and Almond. True dwarf apples are available as of this writing in 1992, but the flavor of the fruit is poor. I am sure that it won't be long before better tasting ones are bred.

ADVANTAGES:

✛ Bear fruit younger.

✛ Bear *more* fruit of a comparable size.

✛ Flower prolifically.

✛ Fine flavor (except apples).

✛ Easy to fence against deer and birds.

✛ Easy to cover with plastic to protect from rain and leaf curl disease in winter.

✛ Can be grown in containers on decks and roof gardens.

✛ Good for miniature espalier.

LIMITATIONS:

✛ Needs yearly pruning for air circulation, because of dense branching. (But you don't need a ladder to do it!)

✛ Must stoop to care for them and/or harvest fruit the first few years.

✛ Fruit is *sometimes* smaller.

✛ Initial cost of the tree is higher.

✛ Only the **newest** varieties have good flavor.

✛ Lifespan may be shorter (i.e. 25 years instead of 100). They haven't been around long enough to know.

✛ Need permanent protection from wildlife (as they will never grow too tall for deer to reach).

Toad's Home in the Garden

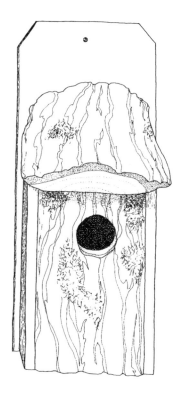

A Screech Owl House

Skunks, shrews, spiders and screech owls. Snakes, toads and frogs, wasps, bats and beetles. All very special friends to a gardener. Without their help we would be up to our proverbial armpits in insects (not to mention mice and rats!). Yet we make their lives very difficult, and in some instances impossible. We kill and shun them, and destroy their habitats instead of encouraging and welcoming them as creatures whose lives make our own more livable.

A single gray bat can eat up to 3000 insects in a night and they are gentle, intelligent creatures that are harmless to man. A toad eats 150,000 insects and slugs in one season and a snake does about the same. All snakes, even the very few poisonous ones, are beneficial to man, keeping the rat, mouse and rabbit population under control. More people are harmed by "Government approved" toxic chemicals than are ever harmed by snakes or spiders. Spider bites are a rare occurrence, and there are very few that are actually poisonous, but the spiders usefulness to mankind is important. As we begin to understand the part wildlife plays in the food "web" we can welcome them into our lives and gardens, and help restore balance to our environments.

THINGS YOU CAN DO TO ENCOURAGE
WILDLIFE IN YOUR YARD

- **Create a meadow or "wild" area.** Mow only once or twice a year, digging out unwanted and overly aggressive plants like Canadian thistle and bindweed.

- **Add a pond.** All creatures drink water, so the addition of a pond, even a tiny one, is worth a thousand plants.

- **Don't rake up dead leaves where you don't need to.**

- **Create a brush pile of prunings in some quiet corner.** It makes a wonderful shelter for small birds and other creatures.

- **Leave an old log or two to rot** and grow moss somewhere in the yard.

- **Plant some large evergreens** if you have room, and leave the ground level branches unpruned. They will provide winter food and shelter for many birds and other critters.

- **Leave some weeds, clover, grasses, and vegetables to go to seed** and feed the wildlife over the winter. You might find some volunteering in early spring eliminating the need to plant.

- **Plant a patch of "bird food"**: sunflowers, buckwheat, millet, grain sorghum. Other wildlings will enjoy it as well. Check with the local State Wildlife agents to see what might be best for your area.

- **Plant a well rounded mix of plants**—evergreen and deciduous shrubs and trees, fruits, herbs, veggies and flowers.

- **Use natives and plants well adapted to your area.**

- **Plant a hedgerow or thicket, using many different plants.** Space plants 5'-8' apart to allow room for growth, and leave them unpruned except to remove some of the oldest wood now and then.

- **Put up bird, bat and owl houses.**

- **Create a small rock pile or rambling rock wall** for habitat, hiding and sunning.

- **Put out a birdbath** and keep it filled with fresh water, especially during very dry spells or very cold spells in winter.

FOR A NEW LOT:

- **Frame the yard** with backdrops of large trees and tall hedges.

- **Create an understory** of small flowering trees planted in groups.
- **Plant shrubs and groundcovers under trees.**

- **Select plants carefully** for the site and for a year-round food supply.

DEER, RABBITS AND RACCOONS

Deer, rabbits and raccoons all have cute and cuddly reputations with everyone except the gardener or farmer who has to compete with them for food or flowers. If these friendly creatures are regular visitors to your yard, you will need to take appropriate measures to protect your plants. Deer will unfortunately nibble happily on many favorite trees and shrubs. They love fruits, veggies and flowers as much as we do, and will make it impossible to grow many plants. Outside of erecting an 8'-9' wire fence or a solid 6' cedar fence around your entire yard, your only option is to confine all their favorites to a single enclosed area. Plant the rest of your landscape with things the deer in your area don't usually consume. Check with your local Extension Service for "deer resistant" lists. Rabbits can usually be kept at bay with a 2' high fence of chicken wire, while an electric wire border is a good deterrent for raccoons.

When the birds you have invited to share your garden start to wipe out your entire crop of blueberries, cherries and grapes, simply throw bird netting over the plants. With a wide variety of food plants available to them, this may never be a problem.

A simple Pond with a shelf for small creatures

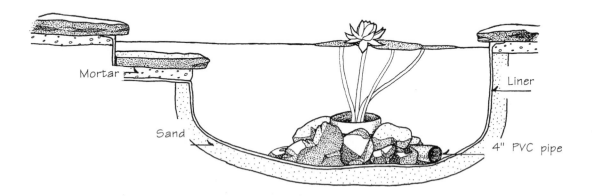

Mortar

Sand

Liner

4" PVC pipe

CREATING A WATER GARDEN

A pool or bird bath of some kind is a charming and practical addition to every garden. Water adds sparkle and beauty, a possible home for aquatic plants, and above all, provides sustenance for birds, butterflies, dragonflies and damselflies, toads, frogs, snakes and all sorts of other wildlife found in a naturally balanced environment.

A source of water can be as simple as a garbage can lid buried to its rim with pebbles on the bottom and plants and rocks around the edge, or a large clay saucer sitting on a stump. To bring fish and water plants into the scene, a sunken half-barrel is an easy and inexpensive home for a water lily and a few goldfish (keep it **above** ground if you have small children around). The new 32 mil plastic pool liners are easy to install. You could build a 6' x 6' pool in a weekend. With the addition of rocks, pebbles, plants and fish, it would fill in and begin to look natural within just a few weeks. A pool such as this quickly develops a natural balance and requires little care beyond adding water occasionally and keeping it free of leaves and other garden debris. Whatever source of water you might choose to create, if it is deeper that 2"-3", be sure to add shallow areas or flat rocks for birds and other small creatures to stand on when they come to bathe and drink.

There are many books that can help you with the creation of a pool, or you may just want to experiment. Even the smallest source of water can add a magical quality to a garden and supply an essential ingredient for the wildlife that will be sharing it with you.

NOTES:

* A *balanced* pond:
    a. demands little care
    b. includes *water, plants* and *fish*; fish keep a pond free of mosquito larvae and plants help keep a pond free of algae by providing shade. They also oxygenate the water and provide cover for the fish.
    c. is clear except for a brief time in early spring and late fall.

STEP BY STEP
Creating a Small Pond

1. Choose an area that can be a focal point of your garden. *Things to consider:* If placed under deciduous trees there will be leaves to deal with in the fall (a screen can be made to cover the pond during leaf fall). If placed under evergreens there will be needles or leaves falling **all year**.

    Full sun is best for water lily bloom, but algae flourishes best in sun as well. (Ultimately, expanding lily and other water plants will shade out most algae over time).

2. Avoid areas where runoff collects. If neighbors use chemicals on their lawn and garden, they may be carried into your pond during heavy rainfall and could be fatal to your fish and plants.

3. Create a safe retreat for fish (from raccoons and cats) by digging one end of your pond at least 2' deep.

4. Create a 1'-2' wide, shallow shelf at one end, to allow access for birds, turtles, salamanders, garter snakes, toads and frogs.

5. Using a carpenter's level strapped to a straight 2"x4" that spans the width of the pond, check the level of the pond rim as you dig. This is most important to the looks of the pond. If one side is higher than another it will always be above the water line (as natural as dark pond liners look under water, they look unpleasantly plastic above water).

6. Clear away sharp objects and line the hole with newspaper or carpet strips.

7. Use the soil from the hole to create a gentle berm or mound around one side if you like.

8. Line the pond with 30-32 mil black or dark green pond liner, fill with water and cover the bottom with small rounded pebbles.

9. Create a safe haven for fish with a 2 foot section of black 4" PVC pipe weighted down by several large rocks.

10. Border the pond with large rocks, low growing and trailing groundcovers and perennials. Mortar any unstable overhanging border rocks in place. Leave room in between for small plants to grow and soften the edges.

11. Add a water lily, several bunches of oxygenating grasses, water snails and several small, inexpensive goldfish. Don't *start out* with expensive fish. Wait at least one season to see how things are working. Plan on feeding the fish 2-3 times a week for the first month or so. Once biological balance is achieved in the pond, feeding will no longer be necessary.

12. Within the first two weeks the pond will develop a heavy algae growth and look a bit like pea soup. DON'T CHANGE THE WATER! This is a natural stage in the process of balancing and if you change the water it will have to start all over. Have patience and within a few weeks clarity will return on its own and remain for the life of the pond, barring any unusual occurrences. Occasionally in the spring and fall algae will be more in evidence, but don't use chemicals to kill it. It is only temporary.

13. Each year after leaf fall in late autumn, clean out any debris that might have accumulated on the pond bottom. Decomposing leaves give off gases that can be hard on fish in very small ponds.

14. Add water periodically to make up for evaporation.

15. With enough good cover to protect them you can expect to see baby fish appearing next spring. Also, with luck, many other small creatures may either take up residence or begin to visit your pond regularly!

The Bench in the Meadow

Butterflies in Your Garden

Butterflies, Beetles, Birds and Bugs

Each year since you started the meadow more have come, fluttering brightly from flower to flower. Now you know their names: Sulphurs and Swallowtails, Monarchs and Blues, Admirals and Fritillaries, Crescents and Whites. Soaring, dipping and gliding over the meadow, fluttering on the flower tops you have lovingly nurtured just for them. You have spent many quiet hours in the little mowed space in the middle of the meadow with the graceful fountain of the Buddleia arching over you in the summer sunshine. It is called the butterfly bush for good reason, sometimes coming alive with small colorful wings fluttering from one tiny purple flower to the next.

It has taken two years for the milkweed to bloom. The type you planted is called butterfly weed and you were sitting quietly under the Buddleia when the Monarch sailed gracefully over the orchard and across the meadow. She made a couple of leisurely circles, surveying the plants there. Finding what she needed, the Monarch settled quietly on a large milkweed. She rested a moment there, then revitalized by the nectar, she began moving gracefully from plant to plant placing on each milkweed a single pearlescent egg—eight in all. Again she rested for a time, on a large dark rock you had placed in the little meadow clearing, warming herself, oblivious to your presence. Seeing her closely you realized she must be nearing the end of her journey, so tattered and dull was she. Then suddenly she was in the air again and soaring up and over the woodland to the north, driven on by some urgent need within her.

The tiny pearly ornaments on the milkweed quickly became minute caterpillars over the next few days. First eating the eggs that held them, they then slowly worked on the leaves from which they had hung. You watched in wonder as these tiny creatures grew, molting four times over the next two weeks, becoming rounded and striped with yellow and black. Of the eight eggs only five made it to this stage and then as you watched, a young starling snatched one from its leaf and carried it off. You knew he would regret this meal and never eat another like it, so sick would the milkweed diet of his caterpillar dinner make him. Even as a butterfly the Monarch would retain within its body the milkweed's toxic chemicals. It's a rare bird that will ever eat two Monarch butterflies, or any butterfly resembling one.

You hadn't been out to the meadow for several days because of the rain and when you went to check on the progress of the four remaining Monarch larvae they were nowhere to be found. You saw instead several black Swallowtails zig-zagging in unison across the meadow. These, you knew from your reading, might have overwintered here in horny brown chrysalides, disguised as a broken twig on a branch in the woodland. You watched a female dotting tips of young Queen Anne's lace plants with her tiny yellow eggs while several others enjoyed the nectar of the clover under the persimmon tree.

Another butterfly had overwintered here hibernating on the willow at the edge of the meadow. The Mourning Cloak, camouflaged against the bark of its tree by large dark wings, rested quietly, lurching into the air at your approach. One morning, on a walk through the woodland, you watched as a group of its bristly, black larvae marched down the willow they had been feeding on since they hatched, each heading to a separate tree to begin the next cycle of their life.

Only a few would make it to adulthood because just the day before a tachina fly had discovered them feeding together on their willow branch and quickly laid a tiny egg on the skin beneath the bristles of all but four of them. Soon the egg would hatch and the tiny grub would make a new home inside its unwilling host.

You and your family watch the dramas of the meadow and woodland, delighting in the swooping antics of the swallows snatching their dinner from the cool evening air. The fat black bumblebee, with its orange leg pouches scurries across the tops of one Queen Anne's lace flower after another, occasionally startling a feeding butterfly with its hurried one-pointedness. Lady bugs feeding on aphids that feed on the milkweed. Ground beetles feeding on grubs feeding on roots. Birds feeding on them all.

Another tiny parasite at work in the meadow is the ichneumon wasp, hardly bigger than a gnat, but capable of keeping the population of Sulphurs and white cabbage butterflies from overwhelming your garden and alfalfa patch. You know the part they play in the gentle life and death struggle that maintains the balance in your meadow and woodland, so you planted and nurtured plants you knew they needed to survive. You love the little golden whirlwinds of the Sulphurs as they swirl across your meadow, but you know that they and the dainty White are among the few butterfly larvae that can do any noticeable damage to your garden. The little ichneumon wasp helps maintain their numbers, with the help of Toad, Snake and the many birds beginning to take up residence here.

Then one day you saw it. Hanging beneath a large milkweed leaf, hidden by the tall grasses around it. An exquisite jade ornament, decorated with little golden discs. Now you knew where the Monarchs larvae had gone. You searched the other milkweed and found two more perfect shining chrysalides. And you wondered how long it would be...

One warm and sunny morning you brought a cup of tea to the little bench under the Buddleia and there hanging from a milkweed leaf nearby, was a newly emerged Monarch, his black and gold wings still limp as wet tissue. You watched in quiet wonder as he turned slowly in the soft morning breeze, drying and testing his new wings, and then climbed tentatively into the sunshine on top of his leaf. A mother bird, heavily burdened by the task of feeding her perpetually hungry brood, was attracted by his flutter and swooped over to investigate. The Monarch, spreading his newly opened wings and springing up at her approach, startled her with his apparent fury and sudden size! She veered off in amazement looking for something smaller and less frightening to feed her waiting youngsters. The Monarch, filled with newly discovered power, soared across the meadow surveying his world from the air--dipping and gliding in delighted abandon.

None of the other chrysalides had survived to bestow their precious contents upon the world. As you lay there in the afternoon sunshine not many days later, watching the Monarch's lazy progress from flower to flower, another black and gold beauty sailed over the orchard and into your meadow. He rose up to meet her, darting around her in the sun. You watched them dancing and diving together, delighting in the discovery of one another until finally they came to rest on a branch at the woodlands edge clinging together quietly for many hours. The next two days you watched the female Monarch deposit her newly fertilized eggs on milkweed around the meadow and then head northward, leaving little pearly droplets in meadows along the way. When she had laid them all, her life would end and the generations after her would make the long migration south before winter settled in.

Since then the butterfly population in your meadow and woodland has grown. Some kinds overwinter here as eggs or pupae and occasionally as adults--bringing to your summer garden color and beauty matched only by the flowers on which they feed. They have added their special magic to your world.

BUTTERFLY MAGIC

Butterflies are such a magical part of a garden (it is said that fairies disguise themselves as butterflies sometimes!) as are birds, beetles and bugs. Many wildflowers and other plants depend on butterflies for pollination: in the Southwest some species of Skippers feed on yucca as larvae and act as the sole pollinator of the plant's flowers when they bloom. Many butterflies are shy and rarely seen by humans, others are friendly and unafraid. Red Admirals will come and sit on your shoulder day after day and Wood Nymphs will follow you down a woodland path. A flower we plant for one will no doubt be enjoyed by many. There is really no way to separate any part of the intricate and complex food web from any other part. So although the focus here is on butterflies and their needs, those things you do for them you do for every life form on the planet.

"Host" Plants for a few common Butterfly larvae

Butterfly	Host Plant
Swallowtail	Umbellifera, Queen Anne's lace, carrot, parsley
Red Admiral	Nettles, woodland trees (birch, wild cherry)
Painted Lady	Thistles, mallow, sunflower, hollyhock
Sulphurs	Legumes (clovers, lupine, birdsfoot trefoil)
Monarch	Milkweed (butterfly weed)
Fritillary	Violets
Mourning Cloaks	Willows
Whites and Orange Tips	Cabbage family and nasturtiums
Crescents	Thistles and asters
Hairstreak	Legumes, oak, mint
Wood Nymph and Satyrs	Grasses
Skippers	Grasses

Some Especially Good *Nectar* Plants

Spring	*Summer*	*Fall*
Lilac	Buddleia	Asters
Mock orange	Butterfly weed	Sedum
Aubrieta	Daisy	Sunflowers
Anemone blanda	Garden *Phlox*	
Rosemary	Coneflowers	
English daisy	Black-eyed susan	
Sweet rocket	Lavender	
Dandelion	Marigolds—single French	
Basket of gold alyssum	Petunias—single	
Arabis—rockcress	Sweet alyssum	
Primrose	Zinnia	

Some Notes on Butterfly Gardening

* **To get them to *come*—**plant a few of their favorite *nectar* plants.

* **To get them to *stay*—**plant food for the larvae, or *"host"* plants.

* **Sunshine is critical for most butterflies.** Put their favorite nectar plants in full sun.

* **Most butterfly caterpillars do little damage to garden plants** because they usually feed singly or in very small groups. The exceptions are: Cabbage butterfly (Whites) larvae, and the larvae of the beautiful black Swallowtail, which are fond of carrot tops, parsley and dill. **Plant a little extra for them**.

* **Garden sprays of all kinds are harmful to butterflies, birds and beneficial insects.**

* **Create a meadow if you can, or a small "wild" garden.** These are the most attractive to butterflies.

* **Plant a good mix of wildflowers and garden flowers.**

* *Fragrant* **flowers appeal to butterflies** just as they do to humans.

* Many butterflies travel only short distances from where they lived as caterpillars—so **plant many** *"host"* **plants as well as** *nectar* **plants.**

* **Water** is an important need in the lives of many butterflies. A birdbath sunk in the ground with a sandy base and beach would be a most welcome feature! Or leave a faucet dripping slowly on a little patch of mud.

* **Provide a little patch of flagstone or a pile of dark rocks for them to sun on.**

* Many of the plants enjoyed by butterflies are appreciated by birds and other beneficial insects as well. **Plant for one and you plant for** *all*!

"Butterflies add another dimension to the garden,
for they are like dream flowers-
childhood dreams-
which have broken loose from their stalks
and escaped into the sunshine"
M. Rothchild

Butterfly on clover

Cabbage and Wild Things

84

Weeds in Your Garden

Weeds and Wild Edibles

You have come to view weeds in a very different light these days! No longer are they just a problem you have to deal with. Now you see some as additions to a spring stir-fry or summer salad and some as butterfly food—either leaves for the larvae or nectar for the adult. Some weeds are useful as parasitic and predator insect food as well. Chickweed and henbit cover bare places in the vegetable garden and protect the soil through the winter. When they aren't feeding you and wildlife the weeds feed the chickens and the compost bin.

A few (although enjoyed by wild creatures) you have determined not to have in your yard or meadow. They are not native to your area and are too aggressive here. These you dig out carefully when they appear. Each year you see fewer of these so your work is not too difficult.

Many weeds—like the wild mustard that blooms in the meadow in spring—are not only tasty greens and buds but lovely in bloom. Tiny beneficial wasps enjoy the nectar and so do early butterflies. You actually transplanted a bit of wild stinging nettle to a place behind the shed. The greens are an important butterfly larvae food and nutritious "people" food as well. Your family really enjoys the cream of nettle soup you make in late spring, and the tender new dandelion greens you serve with vinegar and hard boiled eggs, also home grown!

Wild violets have spread through the woodland and into the meadow path. Fritillary butterfly larvae nibble on the leaves and you use the flowers in spring salads and on birthday cakes! Purslane shows up in the garden every spring along with lamb's quarters and pigweed. Their tender young leaves are as tasty as any garden green and they are much higher in nutrition than most. You have come to consider them valued plants in your garden.

Along the base of your hedgerows you have tucked garden variety flowers—each a close relative to common wildflowers. Poppies, foxglove and iris for late spring bloom, daylilies and yarrow for summer and asters for fall. Weaving through them and in vacant sunny spots all through the yard, the cheerful orange, white and yellow of California poppy, sweet alyssum and nasturtium volunteers tie it all together. Soft blue forget-me-nots fill shady spots where these won't grow. These plants grow in a sort of gay abandon with the wild plants that manage to find empty spots among them. They get water only in long dry spells and are mulched each autumn by falling hedge leaves. You did little to improve the soil here, not wanting these plants to grow lush and large but to evolve to a more natural wildflower-look. Some have done well and others have been quietly crowded out by the stronger and more adaptable. Some grow near the meadow and others border the clover "lawn" in front—all have a friendly and natural look. Some have even wandered into the clover and are mowed once a year. They don't seem to mind.

In the woodland you scattered columbine, primrose, bleeding heart and hosta here and there among the wildlings that already had taken up residence there. You also added little natives that a special nursery nearby sells—wild ginger and wild strawberries and some lovely little ferns. Here you only weed out the odd bramble or stray meadow grass that wanders into a sunny patch and let the rest grow as they will, perhaps moving a shy plant about to be overwhelmed by a more rambunctious one, but interfering as little as possible.

The meadow is your greatest joy. It changes yearly and sometimes you must work to defend your favorite wildflowers from the more aggressive grasses. A meadow is not a truly natural place, as a prairie is. A meadow is actually earth in transition to a forest. In order to keep your meadow what it is you must mow it at least once a year; it is not just an unmown lawn as one might think. Each year you learn new things about your meadow and with its evolution it becomes easier and more "natural" looking. You mow about half of it in a large curving sweep each July and the rest in the fall. This has gently encouraged different plants in each section, adding much needed diversity to your butterfly and insect menu.

Your little patch of lawn near the house is mowed high with the clippings left to feed it and the English daisies, strawberry clover and yarrow have spread delightfully there—creating a little flowery carpet in spring and summer. Violets have crept into the shady end. The new dwarf grasses have nearly taken over the lawn and mowing is often needed only once a month. You overseed it with a bit of flowering lawn mix each fall and perhaps one day they will fill it in completely. Then you can watch the spiders spin webs on your funny old reel mower between mowings!

Weeds have become your allies instead of enemies here and seeing them as friendly companions in your garden has made life ever so much easier for you, just as seeing insects and other wild creatures as a natural and necessary part of your garden has done. This brings you full circle...

Snail and Lily of the Valley

"WEEDS"—LIVING WITH THEM

"Weeds" have a number of useful roles to play in our gardens. They collect and hold nutrients that might otherwise be leached away by rains and sprinklers. They cover and protect the soil, conserving moisture. When they decompose they add important nutrients and organic matter to the soil. Many provide homes or sustenance for insects, butterflies and other wildlife. On top of all that some of the most common are also nourishing and delicious food for humans! Before you rid your landscape of all it s "volunteers", find out who they are and what their role might be.

Maintain a healthy balance by:

    a. **Improving your soil** so your vigorous, healthy plants compete well with any wild plants that do show up.

    b. **Rotating your crops** to disrupt "weed" cycles (disease cycles, too).

    c. **Using mulches, groundcovers and cover crops.** Keep the ground covered.

    d. **Preparing beds 1-2 weeks ahead** and moistening soil to germinate "weed" seeds, then cultivate again.

For very difficult and overly aggressive "weeds" try:

    a. **"Solarizing" the soil;** moistening and covering with clear plastic for several weeks (works best in the southern part of the country or during hot sunny months).

    b. Covering the afflicted area with a **heavy layer of newspaper** (no colored ink) and mulch for several weeks.

    c. **Planting buckwheat** (cut and plant again if necessary).

THE GOURMET "WEEDS"

Edible "weeds" are often the best natural foods because their vigorous root systems supply the plants with more vitamins, minerals and trace elements than their domesticated garden relatives. Pick them young and tender, then use them in salads and stir-fries with your usual greens and they will not only add "spice" to your life but valuable nutrients as well.

PURSLANE

This low-growing perennial has been cultivated as a salad herb in Europe since the 15th century. A recent report from the Weed Science Laboratory of the USDA found purslane contained 6 times the vitamin E in spinach and more omega-3 fatty acid than any other vegetable. As a medicinal plant it is believed to be effective in treating fevers, mixed with honey the plants juices can be used to treat coughs. Native Americans used it for earaches, stomach aches, bruises and burns. It is useful as an ornamental as well, its most popular form being *Portulaca grandiflora* or rose moss. It can be grown in rock gardens, between paving stones or as a lawn substitute for hot dry climates. It prefers a well drained loam so is a common visitor to healthy gardens. It has tiny yellow flowers, thick red stems and succulent leaves. If you find none in your garden try Nichols Garden Nursery.

PIGWEED

Another wild plant that is fond of vegetable and flower beds, this tall annual will bloom from June through August enduring heat and drought. The best flavored greens however are grown with ample water. With the nutritional value of spinach, pigweed leaves have a milder flavor and less oxalic acid. Pigweed and other *Amaranth* relatives have been important food sources in many parts of the world for centuries. The stalks may be eaten like asparagus and the dried seed ground for flour or popped like popcorn. The seed is a fine source of high quality protein, even better than corn or wheat. Several good varieties are available through Peace Seeds. There are many lovely ornamental varieties as well.

LAMB'S QUARTERS or BELGIAN SPINACH
sells for $6.00 a pound in San Francisco. It, too, is a common visitor to gardens because it loves fertile tilled soil. If you find it in your garden you can be assured your soil is good. When turned into the soil, young lamb's quarters plants make a wonderful green manure but be sure to keep a few for eating through the summer. The young diamond-shaped leaves are extremely nourishing with a high content of protein, calcium, iron and vitamins A, B and C (higher than spinach or cabbage!). They are rated the most nutritious green leafy vegetable by the USDA. The seeds are high in protein and make a fine dark flour.

Scientists studying the plant have discovered compounds with many medicinal uses, and there is some thought that it may be the crop of the future although it has been used by many cultures for centuries. Seed can be purchased from Abundant Life Seed Foundation in Washington if you find none in your garden.

CHICKWEED

Common chickweed is a dainty, succulent groundcover, found most commonly in moist shady places in fields and gardens, and makes a wonderful groundcover for empty places in a winter garden. The tiny white flowers bloom from early spring to late fall and the seeds are enjoyed by poultry and birds. Chickweed provides nectar for beneficial wasps and other small insects, and salad greens for humans. The whole plant has too many medicinal uses, internal and external, to be named here, as Native Americans well knew. So if you don't eat it, use it for medicine, or grow it as a groundcover—feed it to your chickens. They will love you! Hence the name *chick*weed.

Weeds in Your Garden 91

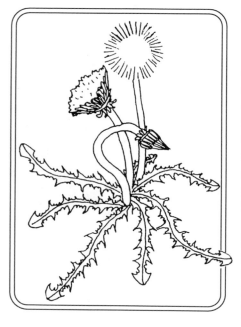

DANDELION

This well known perennial which turns many fields and lawns yellow in the spring, is one of the richest, most versatile and common of all food plants. It ranks just below lamb's quarters, *amaranth* and collard greens in nutritional value. The leaves contain four times more vitamin C than lettuce and have one of the highest contents of vitamin A of any green. The root can be roasted and made into a coffee-like beverage. Its medicinal use has been known for centuries. Herbalists use more dandelion than any other herb as it combines well with other herbs and is safe and wholesome. It is one of China's favorite herbal remedies, used there as a tonic and digestive aid. So the next time you begin to snarl at the dandelions in your early spring lawn, remember their potential value to us all and instead go pick some tender young leaves to add to your spring salad.

This chapter has focused on the usefulness of a few weeds—but the part "wild" plants play in the web of life is as varied as the plants themselves. The point of all this is to help you develop a new attitude toward these "volunteers" in our backyards, and not miss their value because we didn't plant them there ourselves. Nature knows what is needed for balance in a particular site. Become an observer of these wild plants and how they grow, in what conditions they grow, who uses them (of course we won't see bacteria in the soil, night creatures or many shy creatures). Notice the method of growth and reproduction of the weeds that share your space so that you can more easily control the very aggressive ones and leave the rest where they are until you need the space.

"When daisies pied and violets blue,
And lady-smocks all silver-white,
And cuckoo-buds of yellow hue
Do paint the meadows with delight."

Shakespeare

Morning Glory, Queen Anne's Lace and a Visitor

The Lily Pond, the Quince Tree, a wet Robin and a Small Boy

94

Completing Your Plan

Completions

It's been over five years since you and your family put the landscape plan together for your new home. You have followed it carefully, doing some of the work every year and the last bit was put in place a year or so ago. With few exceptions it has all worked well. The trees are beginning to mature and bear fruit or nuts and the groundcovers have spread and filled in their spaces. You tucked perennial flowers in bare spots between young shrubs and now that they have grown the perennials will need to be moved.

Your youngest child has outgrown the swings and sand box, so this summer they will be replaced by a hammock and picnic table. This yard is wonderful for all the children. They seem to have learned more from the process of planning and creating this garden and the work the family has done to encourage wildlife here than all your vacations into the wilds. They have become keen observers and have discovered many fascinating things about your wildlife neighbors on their own. The yard is a special place to many of their friends who spend lazy summer days with your children browsing on all the new and interesting fruits that grow here. They watch beetles in the grass and butterflies in the meadow and discover new birds nesting in the woods. They lay in the shade and watch the fish and pollywogs in the pond, chasing water bugs across the surface.

Your weekends are no longer filled with weeding and mowing chores. Your neighbors and friends watched your progress with interest and considerable skepticism. It soon became apparent that this new kind of garden could not only be less work but beautiful as well. There is something in bloom nearly all year and it all has a comfortable natural loveliness very different from manicured lawns and beds. Your neighbors also began to notice a difference in their "bug" problems after your various wild critters moved in. Obviously these insect eaters weren't confining themselves to your yard alone. Several neighbors have quit using poisons in their yards so they won't endanger the birds and butterflies visiting them now. Your sister and your cousin and their families were so impressed they have been working on achieving the same thing at their homes. And their neighbors have begun to notice. Funny how a good idea spreads... Before long the world could be covered with safe and friendly "backyards" filled with healthy food and happy people and critters...

"Only by looking closely can we begin to understand and appreciate the intimate interrelationships of all living things to one another and to the earth."
S. Olson "The Hidden Forest"

THE FINAL DRAWING

Now that you've been introduced to the basic steps and notions behind the process of putting together a natural, sustainable, low-maintenance, edible landscape and some of its most important elements, it is time to sit down with your lists and your scale drawing and tissue paper and start to put it all on paper.

1. Study your property and its existing features.

2. Place the most important features according to the attention they will need.

3. Place the vegetable garden in an area near the house that gets at least 6 hours of sun. Don't panic if you don't have a large enough sunny area—there are food plants that will grow with some shade, and perhaps you can tuck veggies here and there in small sunny spots around the yard. The FRONT yard is an often un-tapped source of useful space.

4. Place plants according to the sun they need, the room they will need to grow to maturity, and their multiple functions. Go over *"Questions to Ask of Each Plant"* (page 10) and make sure that each is being used to best advantage for you and the plant.

5. Keep it simple and keep the lines flowing in gentle curves.

6. Keep lawn areas to a minimum.

7. Plan everything with the wildlife that will share it in mind.

8. Plan for permanent, weed-proof paths where they are needed.

9. Use a broad range of plants, as **diversity** is an important aspect of a healthy, balanced environment.

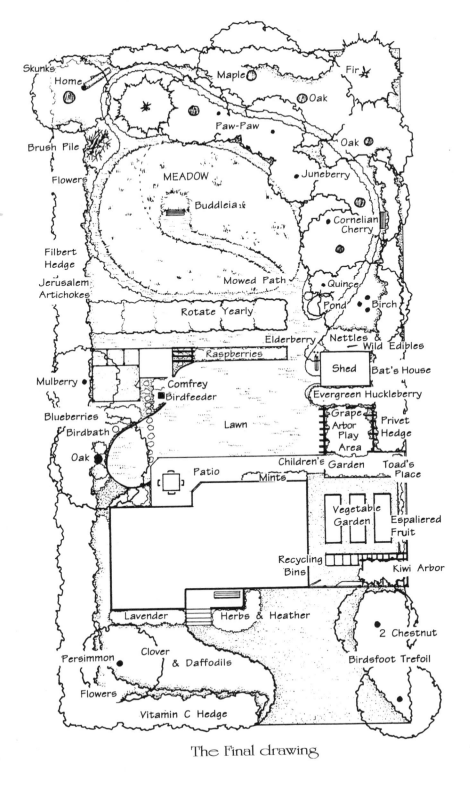

Skunks
Home
Maple
Fir
Oak
Brush Pile
Paw-Paw
Oak
Flowers
Juneberry
MEADOW
Buddleia
Cornelian
Cherry
Filbert
Hedge
Jerusalem
Artichokes
Mowed Path
Quince
Rotate Yearly
Pond
Birch
Elderberry
Nettles &
Wild Edibles
Raspberries
Shed
Bat's House
Mulberry
Comfrey
Birdfeeder
Evergreen Huckleberry
Blueberries
Grape
Arbor
Play
Area
Privet
Hedge
Birdbath
Lawn
Oak
Children's Garden
Toad's
Place
Patio
Mints
Vegetable
Garden
Espaliered
Fruit
Recycling
Bins
Kiwi Arbor
Lavender
Herbs & Heather
2 Chestnut
Persimmon
Clover
& Daffodils
Birdsfoot Trefoil
Flowers
Vitamin C Hedge

The Final drawing

99

By the fruits of our labors shall we be known...

Even those with a small budget or the tiniest of yards will find a way to use some of these ideas. An espaliered fruit tree needs only good soil and a sunny wall or fence, a bird bath takes up little room and a 5 gallon bucket could grow a sunflower and some millet for the birds for winter. A bat house can be tucked under the eaves and a grape vine will shade the smallest outdoor sitting space. Wherever you find yourself at the moment, you have the opportunity to help restore balance and harmony to the planet. You don't need to wait for the "right" place or even wait until you have a place of your own. It doesn't cost money to stop using chemicals on your gardens or encourage your landlord not to. Many landlords would be happy to find alternatives to lawns that are sometimes not mowed and beds that are sometimes not weeded-by tenants uninspired to care. Many annual flowers require little attention and reseed year after year, feeding and giving pleasure to you and many small creatures as well. California poppy, larkspur and sweet rocket are just a few. A handful of sunflower, millet and buckwheat seeds can be saved to replant each year, leaving the majority of the seed on the plants for the birds to enjoy.

And know that whatever steps you choose to take in your life to help restore balance, they will make a difference to all life on the planet—just as a butterfly fluttering its wings affects the air currents around the world.

꒰꒱

"All Nature wears a universal grin"
Henry Fielding

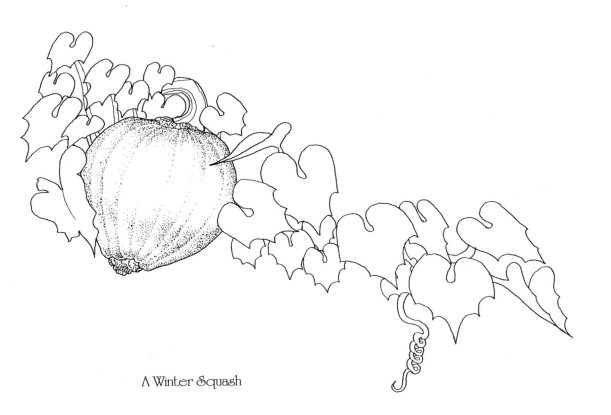

A Winter Squash

The Mower growing Cobwebs in the Shed

Planting & Maintaining Your Garden Naturally

PLANTING & MAINTAINING—*NATURALLY*

The following pages include some simple guidelines for planting and maintaining your "backyard" *naturally*. Many common practices have been tested of late and found to be wanting. Some are based on either the premise that chemical fertilizers and insecticides are good to use or that water and oil are unlimited resources. Both premises have proven to be false. Another common false premise is that all insects and weeds are bad for a garden and need to be eliminated.

These guides are based on our best knowledge to date. As we learn more, I am sure these will change too.

⁊❧

"A woodland walk,
a quest of river-grapes,
a mocking thrush,
a wild-rose or rock-loving columbine,
salve my worst wounds."
Emerson

Whitcomb's Revised Planting Rules

The following is a step by step guide compiled by Prof. Carl Whitcomb of Oklahoma State University after a series of field trials testing traditional methods of tree planting. Please note the emphasis on watering:

1. Select plants *well-adapted* to the soil, light level and micro climates of the site.

2. Make the planting hole as *wide* **as possible**, at least 18 to 24 inches wider than the root ball.

3. If the spade has glazed the sides of the hole, *break up the compacted soil.*

4. Fill the hole with the *same soil* removed from the hole. *Don't mix amendments with the soil.*

5. To get rid of air pockets, *water as you backfill*. If you tread the soil around the tree or shrub, tread lightly.

6. *Water several hours after planting* and again **every 7-10 days** for the first season.

7. *Mulch heavily* five to seven feet out from trees, three to four feet from shrubs. Mulch three to four inches deep using barkdust or compost.

8. *Prune as little as possible.* Remove only damaged branches. Prune for shape after the plant is well-established.

9. *Stake only if necessary* (for trees with very large canopies).

10. Fertilize immediately after planting and again the next fall after leaf drop. *Use slow release organic fertilizer.* Apply only to *soil surface.*

Revised tree planting techniques in a nut-shell

PLANT IN *UNAMENDED* SOIL. A tree or shrub planted in unamended soil adjusts quickly and makes steady, uninterrupted progress. A tree planted in soil with compost, manure or peat moss and fertilizers added to the planting hole may start out well. But as soon as new roots hit the unamended soil surrounding the planting hole, it is often severely set back.

STAKING OFTEN NOT NECESSARY. Except when planting large trees with broad canopies, field trials have shown most young trees do better *without staking*. The natural air movement encourages strong root growth.

EARLY PRUNING DOES MORE HARM THAN GOOD. The common practice of top pruning a tree or shrub to make up for root loss in transplanting actually stimulates **more** top growth at the expense of root growth. Remove only damaged branches at planting.

MULCH—AN IMPORTANT GARDEN TOOL

In nature, the surface of the soil is usually covered by living plant material or plant debris—leaves, needles and dying plants. In our yards and gardens, we often maintain areas of bare soil between plants, especially in vegetable and annual flower beds. A 2"-5" layer of organic mulch is a fine imitation of natural conditions and offers the following benefits:

+ **Insulates the soil**—protecting surface roots.

+ **Cuts down on watering needs**—maintains moisture in soil, slows down evaporation.

+ **Keeps soil from crusting**—reduces erosion and compaction by rain and sprinklers.

+ **Keeps weeds down**—practically eliminates weeding chores and makes those weeds that do grow easier to pull.

+ **Supplies humus and nutrients**—improves soil structure over time as soil organisms work the bottom layer of mulch into the soil beneath.

+ **Prevents muddy splash**—on greens and other low plants.

+ **Prevents rot and spread of fungal diseases** by splashing water—keeps vegetables and fruits off damp ground.

WHEN NOT TO MULCH:

+ **When your soil is poorly drained** and stays wet and cold all season, plant groundcovers instead, to soak up moisture.

+ Uncover vegetable and annual flower beds early in spring to allow time for the soil to dry out and warm up.

WATERING PRACTICES REVIEWED

Nearly half our water comes from groundwater, and since the early 1900's we have been consuming this reserve faster than it can be naturally replenished. Add to this increasing periods of drought and the future could find us dealing with a serious water shortage. If we start now—taking measures in our own "backyard"—perhaps this bleak prediction for the future might be averted.

POOR WATER USAGE:

- Frequent shallow watering
- Watering during the hottest part of the day
- Overwatering to the point of run-off
- Watering on windy days
- Installing lawns on slopes where there is run-off
- Large areas of lawn
- Hosing down patios, decks, driveways and sidewalks
- Overhead watering—sprinklers

WATERING GUIDE

Water deeply and infrequently—soak soil to a minimum of 6 inches. Deep watering encourages deep roots.

Water during the cool parts of the day on still days.

Use drip or "ooze" soaker hose irrigation where possible.

Mulch heavily—Lay irrigation system under mulch. Mulch retains water and prevents soil from drying out.

Check water penetration periodically by digging holes around yard after watering.

LAWN MAINTENANCE GUIDE

▼ **When initially planting look for new dwarf and drought-tolerant varieties and flowering lawn mixes.** Also consider sowing seed at a 50-65% lower rate than recommended—for healthier plants.

▼ **Don't use chemical fertilizers or herbicides on your lawn.** They kill microbes in the soil and drive off earthworms and other useful soil critters.

▼ **Mow regularly.** Cut to a *minimum* of 2" in spring and fall, and 3" in summer. Keep the mower blades sharp to avoid ripping the grass.

▼ **Leave the grass clippings.** They add nitrogen back to the lawn. Thatch is not a buildup of grass clippings as many suppose. It is more often due to the use of chemical fertilizers and their detrimental effect on soil life and tilth.

▼ **Water deeply when dry.** Infrequent, deep waterings create deep-rooted grass that is able to withstand some drought. Water once every week or two when the weather is warm and sunny and there has been less than an inch of rain.

▼ **Hand weed when needed.** A thick, healthy lawn kept at 3" tall will shade and crowd out most weeds.

▼ **Top-dress every year or so.** Broadcast a half inch layer of fine, screened organic matter (compost or aged manure) over the lawn in the fall.

▼ **Aerate older lawns every 3 to 4** years if needed—with a machine that removes plugs of soil. Top dress with compost or manure as usual. Water well.

▼ **Test soil pH every two years** and spread lime as needed to sweeten soil. This step alone will often release nutrients bound up by the acidity in the soil.

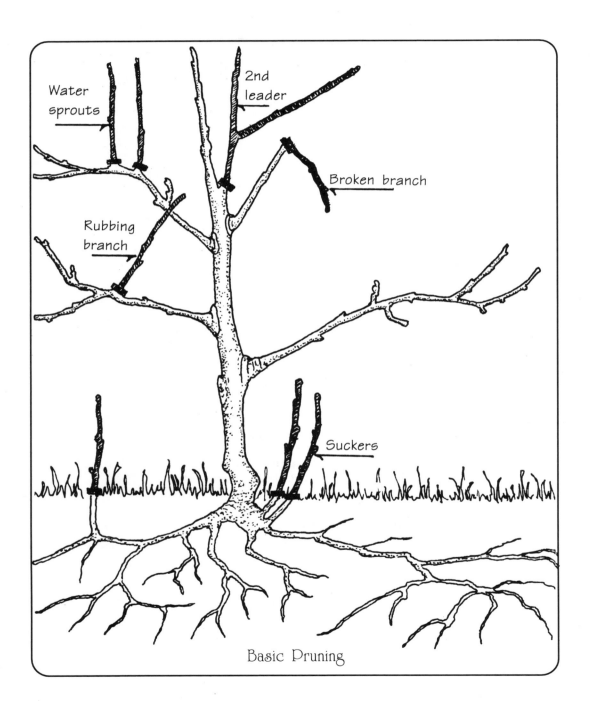

Basic Pruning

PRUNING

Careful plant selection and placement—taking a plant's possible ultimate size and cultural needs into consideration—can eliminate the need for much unnecessary pruning. Different techniques are needed for different types of plants, so before you approach your tree, shrub or vine with pruning shears, take a little time to find out what will work best for that particular plant. The following are some very basic guidelines:

- Prune most deciduous trees and shrubs while dormant.
- Prune flowering shrubs right after blooming.
- Remove any dead or damaged wood and shape where needed.
- Don't leave long stubs that can rot and cause disease.
- For bushier growth remove the terminal bud.
- Remove suckers and water sprouts (see drawing).
- Don't use pruning paint on the cuts. Studies show wounds heal better if left unpainted.
- Remove any crowded or rubbing branches (see drawing).
- Rinse pruning tools in bleach solution to kill any disease organisms that might be carried from plant to plant.

TO LIMIT TREE SIZE:

- Summer prune (no *winter* prune).
- Prune to two-year old wood.
- Cut out vigorous limbs and shoots.
- Create a long distance from the ground to the lowest branches.
- Encourage heavy fruiting (this uses *growing* energy).
- Plant trees close together.
- Use competitive groundcover.
- Limit water and fertilizer.
- Prune to horizontal branches.
- Plant in heavy clay soil.
- Plant graft union high above the soil.

NO-PRUNE STYLE

Terminal-bearing fruit trees such as quince, walnut, persimmon, mulberry, fig, pomegranate, loquat, chestnut and cane fruit—where the flowers form on the new growth—can often be maintained with little or no pruning at all. Remove only crowded, rubbing or broken branches, suckers, dead or damaged wood.

ADVANTAGES:

* More fruit
* Less work

DISADVANTAGES:

* Less reachable fruit as tree ages
* Uneven color
* Smaller fruit (might be an *advantage*)
* Alternate-year bearing on some trees
* Sometimes not as attractive
* Broken limbs can occur from heavy cropping

INSECTS AND DISEASES

INSECTS

Plants have surprisingly efficient and sophisticated defenses against insect attack, especially when they are kept strong and healthy with sufficient amounts of food, water, and sunlight, and have enough room to grow well. Weak plants, like people, have less resistance than healthy ones and can even *attract* insects.

Some things we can do to help plants defend against insects are:

   ◆*MAINTAIN BALANCED GROWTH* by incorporating liberal amounts of organic matter into the soil and foliar feeding occasionally with liquid seaweed or fish emulsion.

   ◆*DIVERSIFY*—grow a large variety of plants. We are just learning some of the more useful relationships of various plants and insects. Experiment and be observant of natural balances.

   ◆*NEVER USE STRONG CHEMICALS* on your property. They may kill predators and stimulate resistance in pests.

   ◆*ENCOURAGE PREDATORS*—wasps, birds, spiders, etc. A bird bath or small pond is good for attracting helpful wild critters.

ABOVE ALL—Recognize that the more loving and harmonious an atmosphere we create in our yards, the less imbalance will occur. Keep in mind also, that all living organisms have their place (that spider you may be tempted to kill works hard to keep the pest population in your yard and house under control).

REMEMBER—returning your home grounds to a natural, balanced state does not happen overnight. It may take two or more years to accomplish, depending on what conditions you are starting with and how quickly you are able to add to the environment those aspects necessary for balance.

⌘ INSECT GUIDE ⌘

Should you be subject to a heavy insect attack of some kind, try not to panic. It happens now and then in the most balanced environments. Insects can eat a lot before they do any real harm. Therefore:

❖ **FEED YOUR PLANTS**—a compost topdressing and a foliar feed will help a plant's resistance.

❖ **FEED THE BUGS**—if only a small percentage of your crop is affected, leave well enough alone and give predators time to colonize. They may take care of the problem for you.

❖ **FOCUS ON THE PROBLEM**—many larger bugs can be controlled by hand-picking for a few days, and the smaller insects can often be discouraged with sprays of water.

❖ **BIOLOGICAL CONTROLS**—if it's a leaf or fruit-eating larvae (cabbage worm, etc.) consider using *Bacillus thuringiensis* or other bacillus, which are harmless to humans, animals, and beneficial insects.

Above all, learn to tolerate some insects in your yard. Remember—concentrate on building healthy soil for healthy plants.

Lacewing and Ladybug

❖ DISEASE ❖

Plant diseases have much more potential for damage to our landscapes than do insects, and are much more difficult to control once they strike. For this reason most control strategies are of a **preventive** nature:

❖ *RESISTANT PLANTS AND PLANT VARIETIES:*

Study garden encyclopedias, seed and plant catalogs, and talk to nursery people and horticulturists when planning additions to your garden. **Choose those plants found to be the most resistant to disease in your climate.**

❖ *CULTURAL TECHNIQUES:*

In the vegetable garden, rotating your crops (not planting the same vegetable family in the same spot 2 years in a row) is a good disease avoidance procedure. **Good air circulation** is important to many types of plants. **Avoid overhead watering** *late in the day*. Plant leaves that stay damp all night develop fungal diseases more readily. Diseased plants should not be left around the yard or put in the compost. Burn them or put them in the garbage.

CLOSING

For all the relaxed gardeners among us who have a tendency to let things get a bit weedy and critter-munched anyway, this book will be a vindication for your style of gardening. But for those who are naturally tidy and meticulous, much that has been put forth here may be difficult to swallow. Your large expanse of utterly weed-free lawn may be your pride and joy. My mother is such a gardener and spends many hours each year with a butter knife prying any invading weed out of their lovely lawn. Switching to one of the new dwarf drought-tolerant flowering lawn mixes now coming on the market will not only cut down on your time expenditure but on the use of other resources as well. (Not to mention wear and tear on your butter knives!).

Be encouraged to make use of wasted front and side yards in new ways. We once lived in a house that had no backyard. We put a high fence around much of the front and side in order to have some privacy and grew vegetables and fruits both inside and outside the fence. A long strip next to our quiet dead end street was planted with potatoes, corn, squash, bird food, etc. and dwarf fruit trees were espaliered on the outside of the fence. Grapes over a sitting area, kiwis along the top of the fence on one side and blueberries marching up the entry path, together with a flower-filled vegetable garden to the side, gave us a lovely and productive garden even though it was only about 30'x60'. Neighbors walking by often commented on how pleasant it was to watch its progress through the seasons and neighborhood children would watch in wonder as we unearthed a treasure trove of potatoes!

I hope you are encouraged to try a bit of "wild" gardening, especially if you have an area that can be screened in some way from the rest of the yard. We once had a very deep back yard that we developed and planted heavily in the area nearest the house first. A large basically unlandscaped area was separated from this by a bed of shrubs and a filbert tree and after a failed attempt at naturalizing annual flowers there we just mowed what came up once every month or so and put in a fire pit. Around the perimeter we planted perennials divisions from overcrowded beds near the house. The hose didn't reach this area so it only got rainwater, and weeds wandered among the flowers. This soon became our favorite place to drag our chairs in the evening and if it was cool, we would bring a log or two and build a small fire in the little stone edged pit. The weeds didn't seem out of place here weaving among the perennials and the ground was a carpet of low flowering "weeds" that didn't mind being mowed now and then. Birds and butterflies abounded here and one could truly relax after a long hard day. From here you could see no weeds that needed pulling or lawn that needed mowing or plants that needed pruning or watering. It was a place of tranquillity and harmony—a place to just "be".

I hope this book inspires you to create a space like that for yourself as well— think of all the critters you will benefit in the process! I hope more than anything this book encourages a new view of our relationship to our gardens and all the other life forms that can and do inhabit them. May we all once more become partners with nature, working in loving harmony to add to the quality of life on the planet for us all—*starting with our own backyards.*

Birdsfoot trefoil

"Ye marshes, how candid and simple
and nothing-with-holding and free,
ye publish yourselves to the sky
and offer yourselves to the sea".

Sidney Lanier

Wild Iris & Wild Rose

APPENDICES

GLOSSARY

ORGANIC FERTILIZER GUIDE

USEFUL LISTS:
      Low-Care Edibles
      Native Nuts
      Insect and Disease-Resistant Edibles
      Shade-Tolerant Edibles
      Drought-Tolerant Edibles and Ornamentals
      Edible Flowers

SOURCES

FURTHER READING

PERIODICALS AND ORGANIZATIONS

GLOSSARY

Amendment - A substance added to the soil to improve structure or fertility.

Annual - A plant with a life cycle that is completed in one year or season.

Biennial - A plant that completes its life cycle in two years, usually blooming and going to seed and dying the second season.

Cover crop - A crop grown to prevent or reduce erosion. When it is turned into the soil it acts as a green manure.

Deciduous - A plant that sheds its leaves at the end of the growing season.

Drought resistant - Plants that do well with very little water.

Drought tolerant - Plants that survive drought by going dormant or some similar tactic.

Edibles - Plants with some part that is safe to be eaten by humans or animals.

Espalier - A tree or shrub trained to grow on a flat surface, such as a wall or fence.

Green Manure - Any crop grown to be tilled or turned into the soil, thereby adding organic matter, increasing absorption and the biochemical processes. An inexpensive way to fertilize, improve and protect the soil. Also provide nectar for bees and other insects, nutrition for worms and disruption of weed cycles. Many green manures will break up heavy soils.

Humus - The decayed plant and animal material in the soil.

Mulch - a layer of material spread on the soil surface to conserve moisture, hold down weeds, improve soil structure, and protect from freezing. Commonly used materials include straw, dried grass clippings, leaves, ground bark, sawdust, pine needles, and wood chips.

Natives - Plants, animals or insects living or occurring naturally in an area.

"Ooze" watering system - Black soaker hose made from recycled tires spun in a way that allows water to "ooze" from pores in the surface. May be connected by sections of solid hose or PVC pipe and PVC connections to create a watering system similar to the more common "sprinkling" systems. Can and should be buried 2"-6" below soil surface for best water use and protection of hose from ultraviolet rays. Wonderful for raised vegetable beds and other heavily planted areas.

Overwintering crop - Normally a vegetable crop that either comes to maturity in late fall and survives and is harvested throughout the winter, or a crop that is started in early fall and goes through winter as a young plant. The latter matures and is harvested in early spring when the weather begins to warm. Many cool weather crops may be treated this way, allowing for much earlier harvests than possible with spring sowing.

Perennial - An herbaceous plant that persists from year to year, for three or more years.

Self-seeding - Plants that drop seeds that commonly and easily grow into new plants, sometimes the same year, more often the next spring. Sweet alyssum, nasturtiums, calendulas, California poppy, and forget-me-not are common self-seeders in the Pacific Northwest and many northern states.

Sucker - A shoot growing from the base of a plant.

Tilth - The structure and texture of the soil.

ORGANIC FERTILIZER CHART

Type	Rate per 1000 sq. feet	Duration	Use	Main Nutrient
Composted animal manure	300-500 lbs.	2-3 years	soil builder, lawn dressing, mulch	Nitrogen and Phosphorous
Compost	up to 300 lbs.	2-3 years	organic matter fertilizer	humus and many nutrients according to its composition
Bloodmeal	varies with soil needs*	1-4 months	lawns and groundcovers	Nitrogen and protein
Bonemeal	varies with soil needs*	2-5 years	veggies and fruit bulbs	Phosphorous and Nitrogen
Rock phosphate	varies with soil needs*	2-5 years	Phosphate for fruit and veggies	Phosphorous
Greensand	varies with soil needs*	2-5 years	soil builder with trace elements	Potassium
Dolomite Lime	varies with soil needs- test pH*	2-5 years	sweetens (lowers acidity) and conditions soil	secondary nutrients pH balance
Fish Emulsion	1-2 tbsp./ gal. water	every 2 weeks	seedlings transplants houseplants	Nitrogen and Phosphorous
Liquid Seaweed	1 tbsp./gal. water	every 2 months	good foliar feed lawns and seedlings houseplants	trace nutrients
Dried Seaweed	¼-½ cup/ gal.water	every 2 months	good foliar feed lawns and seedlings houseplants	trace nutrients

*A soil test will determine the quantities needed for your soil

USEFUL LISTS

ESPECIALLY LOW-CARE FRUITS

TREES	SHRUBS	PERENNIALS
Nanking cherry	Pineapple guava	Alpine strawberry
Jujube	Blueberries	All edible groundcovers
Cornelian cherry	Pomegranate	listed
Raisin tree		

All **native** trees, shrubs and perennials—in their *natural areas.*

NATIVE AMERICAN NUT TREES

Pecan	Beech	Hickory	
Butternut	Hazelnut	Pine	Oak

INSECT AND DISEASE-RESISTANT EDIBLES

Some varieties of *all* types of edible plants have been bred for insect and disease resistance.

TREES	SHRUBS	PERENNIALS
Chestnuts	Beach plum	Alpine strawberry
Elderberry	Blueberry	Wild strawberry
Fig	Bush cherry	Daylily
Quince	Nanking cherry	Sage
Persimmon	Rugosa rose	Thyme
Black walnut	Blackberry	Wintergreen
	Pineapple guava	Salal
	Rosa pomifera	
	Black raspberry	
	Wild gooseberry	

SHADE TOLERANT EDIBLES

Shade Tolerant Perennials	Shade Tolerant Annuals
Alpine and wild strawberries	Basil
American Persimmon	Beans
Some bamboo	Beets
Bee balm	Borage
Blueberry	*Calendula*
California bay laurel	Celery
Comfrey	Chard
Currant	Chervil
Daylily	Cress
Echinacea	Endive
Elderberry	Kale
Goldenseal	Lamb's quarters
Gooseberry	Leaf lettuce
Evergreen Huckleberry	Nasturtiums
Kiwi "Arctic Beauty"	Nettles
Lovage	Parsnips
Mints	Peas
Oregon grape	Potatoes
Primrose	Pumpkins
Redwood sorrel	Quinoa
Rhubarb	Radishes
Salal	Rutabagas
Stinging nettle	Salsify
Sorrel	Squash
Sweet cicely	Turnips
Sweet woodruff	
Sweet violet	
Valerian	
Wintergreen	
Wood betony	

DROUGHT-TOLERANT PLANTS

Edibles

Trees	Shrubs/Perennials	Annuals
Chestnuts	Grape	Amaranths
Fig	*Rosa Rugosa*	Corn (some varieties)
Almond	Autumn olive	Grains (some varieties)
Black locust	Bearberry/kinnikinnick	Salvia
Mulberry	Pineapple guava	***End of Season:***
Sand cherry	Pomegranate	Beans—drying kinds
Dwarf redleaf plum	Rosemary	Chili peppers
Hollyleaf cherry	Thymes	Tomatoes
Chinese pistache	Sages	Onions
Pine	*Aloe*	Garlic
Turkish tree hazel	*Echinacea* (coneflower)	Melons
Peach	Oregon grape	Sunflowers
Chinese jujube		
Eucalyptus		
Mesquite		
Oak		

DROUGHT-TOLERANT PLANTS

Ornamentals

Trees	Shrubs	Perennials/Annuals	
Acacia--many kinds	Firethorn	*Acanthus Mollis*	*Penstemon*
Incense cedar	Sumac	*Agapanthus*	Matilija poppy
Catalpa	Snowberry	*Agave*	Sea Pink
Palo Verde	*Aucuba japonica*	Pussytoes	*Santolina*
Western redbud	Siberian peashrub	Black-eyed susan	*Sedum*
Ginkgo	*Ceanothus*	*Artemisia*	Rue
Hackberry	Cotoneaster	Butterfly weed	Dusty miller
Eleagnus	Broom	False indigo	Germander
	Crepe myrtle	Trumpet vine	Wisteria
	Hibiscus	Red valerian	Yarrow
	Potentilla	Snow-in-summer	*Yucca*
	Yew	*Coreopsis*	
		Pampas Grass	
		Blanket flower	
		Sneezeweed	
		Iris	
		Lantana	
		Sea lavender	
		Flax	
		Honeysuckle	
		Evening primrose	
		Oriental poppy	
		Fountain grass	

EDIBLE FLOWERS

Apple blossom
Bee balm
Calendula
Carnations
Cattail
Chamomile
Chickweed
Chicory
Chives
Chrysanthemum
Red clover
Comfrey
Daisy
Dandelion
Daylily
Dill
Elderberry blossom
Gladiolus
Goldenrod
Hawthorn
Honeysuckle
Hyssop
Jasmine
Johnny-Jump-Up
Hollyhock

Lavender
Lemon balm
Lemon blossom
Lemon verbena
Lilac
Mallow
Marjoram
Mullein
Mustard
Nasturtium
Oregano
Pansy
Passion flower
Petunia
Plum blossom
Poppy
Primrose
Rose
Rosemary
Sage
Squash blossom
Sweet woodruff
Thyme
Violet
Yucca

SOURCES LISTS

SEEDS   * indicates companies that sell only UNTREATED seed

Abundant Life Seed Foundation*, P.O. Box 772, Port Townsend, WA 98368

Peace Seeds* (**organic** seeds) Deep Diversity Catalog, Box 190, Gila, NM 88038

Seeds of Change* (**organic** seeds), 621 Old Santa Fe #10, Santa Fe, NM 87501

Seed Savers Exchange* (Share rare and endangered seeds), 3076 North Winn Rd., Decorah, IA 52101 (319)382-5990 $1 membership brochure

Nichols Garden Nursery*, 1190 N. Pacific Highway, Albany, OR 97321

Ecogeneses Inc.*, 16 Jedburgh Road, Toronto, ONT Canada M5M 3J6

Southern Exposure Seed Exchange*, P.O. Box 158, North Garden, VA 22959

Bountiful Gardens*(open-pollinated seed), 18001 Shafer Ranch Rd., CA 95490

Down On The Farm Seed*(open-pollinated seed), P.O. Box 184, Hiram, OH 44234

Garden City Seeds*(**organic**, open-pollinated seed), 1324 Red Crow Road, Victor, MT 59875 Nonprofit group.

Johnny's Selected Seeds, Foss Hill Road, Albion, MA 04910

Territorial Seed Co., P.O. Box 157, Cottage Grove, OR 97424

Tillinghast Seed Co., P.O. Box 738, La Connor, WA 98257

Hobbs & Hopkins, (Fleur de Lawn), 1712 SE Ankeny, Portland, OR 97214

WILDFLOWERS—Plants and Seeds

Natural Legacy Seeds, RR 2, C-1 Laird, Armstrong, BC, Canada VOE 1B0
Seed- Free price list

Appalachian Wildflower Nursery, Route 1, Box 275A, Reedsville, PA 17084
Plants- $2 Catalog or free list for 1 first class stamp.

Las Pilitas Nursery, Star Rt. Box 23X, Santa Margarita, CA 93453
Plants and Seed- Free price list, $4 Catalog

Lofts Seed Inc., Chimney Rock Road, Bound Brook, NJ 08805
Seed- Free price list

Native American Seed, 3400 Long Prairie Road, Flower Mound, TX 75028
Seed- $1 Catalog

Niche Gardens, 1111 Dawson Road, Chapel Hill, NC 27516
Plants- $3 Catalog

Prairie Moon Nursery, Route 2, Box 163, Winona, MN 55987
Plants and Seeds- $2 for 2 year catalog subscription

Prairie Nursery, P.O. Box 306, Westfield, WI 53964
Plants and Seed- $3 for a 2 year catalog subscription

The Fragrant Path, P.O Box 328, Fort Calhoun, NE 68023
Seed- $1 Catalog

The Vermont Wildflower Farm, Dept. OG, Route 7, Charlotte, Vt. 05445
Seed- Free Catalog

ORGANIC SUPPLIES

Harmony Farm Supply, P.O. Box 460, Graton, CA 95444

Peaceful Valley Farm Supply, P.O. Box 2209, Grass Valley, CA 95945

Necessary Trading Co., New Castle, VA 24127

Ringer Research, 6860 Flying Cloud Dr., Eden Prairie, MN 55344

Smith and Hawkin, 25 Corte Madera, Mill Valley, CA 94941

Gardener's Supply Co., 133 Elm St. Winooski, VT 05301

Wild Bird Centers of America, Inc. Suppliers of birding products. Main office— 7687 MacArthur Blvd., Cabin John, MD 20818. Many stores located throughout North America. Call *1-800-759-WILD* for the address of the center nearest you.

FURTHER READING

Wildlife in your garden Gene Logsdon 1983
Rodale Press, Emmaus, PA

Uncommon Fruits Worthy of Attention, a Gardeners Guide Lee Reich 1991 Addison-Wesley Publishing Co. Inc.

Worms Eat my Garbage Mary Appelhof 1982
Flower Press, Kalamazoo, MI

Earthly Delights Rosalind Creasy 1985
Sierra Club Books, Yolla Bolly Press

The Country diary Book of Creating a Butterfly Garden E.J.M. Warren 1988
Henry Holt and Co. Inc. N.Y., NY

Bright Wings of Summer David G. Measures 1976
Prentice-Hall, Inc. Englewood, NJ

The Audubon Society Handbook for Butterfly Watchers Robert Michael Pyle 1984
Charles Scribner's Sons, NY

Wings in the Meadow Jo Brewer 1967
Houghton Mifflin Company, Boston, MA

Indian Herbology of North America Alma R. Hutchens 1969
Merco, Ontario, Canada

The Encyclopedia of Organic Gardening Organic Gardening Magazine Staff 1978
Rodale Press, Emmaus, PA

Sunset Western Garden Book Editors of Sunset Magazine and Sunset Books 1967
Lane Magazine and Book Co. Menlo Park, CA

Designing and Maintaining your Edible Landscape Naturally Robert Kourik 1986
Rodale Press, Inc., 33 E. Minor, Emmaus, PA 18049

Landscaping with Wildflowers: An Environmental Approach to Gardening Jim Wilson 1992 Houghton Mifflin Publishing

Dan's Practical Guide to Least Toxic Home Pest Control   Dan Stein   1991
Hulogosi, Eugene, OR

Low-Maintenance Gardening   Editors of Sunset Books and Sunset Magazine   1974
Lane Books, Menlo Park, CA

The Chemical-Free Lawn   Warren Schultz   1989
Rodale Press, Emmaus, PA

Natures Design   Carol A. Smyser and editors of Rodale Press Books   1982
Rodale Press, Emmaus, PA

The New American Landscape Gardener   Phebe Leighton and Calvin Simonds
1987   Rodale Press, Emmaus, PA

Cornucopia   S. Facciola   1990
Kanpong Press, Vista CA

PERIODICALS AND ORGANIZATIONS

Avant Gardener
Horticultural Data Processers
P.O. Box 489
New York, NY 10028

Harrowsmith Country Life
Ferry Rd.
Charlotte, VT 05445

Rodale's Organic Gardening
33 East Minor
Emmaus, PA 18049

Mother Earth News
24 E. 23rd St.
NY, NY 10010

Nature Conservancy
1815 North Lynn Street,
Arlington, VA 22209

Greenpeace
1436 U Street NW
Washington, D.C. 20090

Native Seeds/Search
3950 W. New York Dr.
Tuscon, AZ 85745

National Wildflower Research Center
2600 FM 973 North
Austin, TX 78725
$2 plant list tailored to your area

INDEX

All garden store, gift shop and natural food store inquiries
may be made to:

Down To Earth Distributors,
345 Lincoln Street Alley,
Eugene, OR 97401
Phone: (503) 485-5932

Please direct bookstore and library inquiries to:

Pacific Pipeline, Inc.
8030 South 228th Street,
Kent, WA 98032-3898
Phone: (206) 395-1525

Holistic Garden Products

To help keep the spirit of the holistic garden alive we have made available to you a poster and T-shirt **from the cover art of The Holistic Garden!**

Included on the poster and T-shirt is a quote by Naturalist John Muir:

"When we tug at a single thing in nature, we find it attached to the rest of the world."

18"x 24" poster is printed on recycled paper with soy ink. The T-shirt is white 100 % cotton.

Please send

Quantity	Size	Item	Price ea.	
	M	The Holistic garden T-shirt	$ 16.50	
	L	The Holistic garden T-shirt	$ 16.50	
	XL	The Holistic garden T-shirt	$ 16.50	
	XXL	The Holistic garden T-shirt	$ 18.50	

Quantity	Item	Price ea.	
	The Holistic garden Poster	$ 15.00	
		Total $=	

Please include $2.00 postage

Send to:

Name _____

Address _____

_____

Send check or money order to: Mandala Arts
3960 Blanton Road Eugene, OR 97405
Or call 1-800-344-8072

notes

2917007